THE PRINCE OF WALES: RIGHT OR WRONG?
AN ARCHITECT REPLIES

Maxwell Hutchinson was born in 1948 in Grantham, Lincolnshire, the son of an architect. He studied at the Scott Sutherland School of Architecture in Aberdeen and the Architectural Association School of Architecture in London. He founded Hutchinson and Partners, Chartered Architects, in 1972. The practice's work is now wide in scope, including maintenance, rehabilitation and repair of inner-city housing, estate security, housing and office developments, and large-scale urban regeneration projects.

He joined the Royal Institute of British Architects (RIBA) in 1972. He was Chairman of the North East Thames Branch from 1975 to 1977 and of the London Region from 1979 to 1981. He has been the Chairman of their Energy Policy Committee, the National Conferences in 1982 and 1983, and the London Environment Group. He was elected Senior Vice President by the Council in 1988 and became President in July 1989.

The Prince of Wales: Right or Wrong?
An architect replies

MAXWELL
HUTCHINSON

faber and faber

LONDON · BOSTON

First published in 1989
by Faber and Faber Limited
3 Queen Square London WC1N 3AU

Phototypeset by Input Typesetting Ltd, London
Printed in Great Britain by
Richard Clay Ltd, Bungay, Suffolk

A CIP record of this book is available
from the British Library

ISBN 0-571-14287-7
ISBN 0-571-14180-3 (Pbk)

Contents

The Prince and the Architect

In a democracy it is extremely difficult to argue with the heir to the throne. Max Hutchinson has taken on the establishment and the millions who follow every move of our Royal Family as they are closely pursued by the media. His book challenges the popular view that architects are solely to blame for the poor state of our built environment and that architecture can be considered in isolation from the prevailing political, economic, artistic and technological background. In arguing for modernism it attacks the myth that the way forward into the twenty-first century is rooted in the revival of the past – 'a form of backing into the future'.

Modernism includes a recognition of history and the need to conserve beautiful buildings – though not all old buildings are beautiful any more than all modern buildings are.

Hope in the future is rooted in the memory of the past; without memory there is no history and no knowledge. No projection of the future can be formed without reference to the past. Past, present and future, memory and prophecy are woven together into one continuous whole, so that in the understanding of the past lies the hope of the future. However, the nostalgic copying of past forms and the mindless conservation of all that was built before this century will destroy the rich potential that lies in the future and cities will become museums. Building of little cultural worth may be demolished so that renewal can take place.

Departure from tradition has always provoked ferocious controversy and opposition. At the opening of the new Lloyd's building by the Queen, the Dean of St Paul's, noting that I was looking beleaguered, reminded me of the opposition that Wren had encountered in the construction of St Paul's. Apparently, he had had to build a wall eighteen feet high around the site to prevent his critics from seeing and once more frustrating his plans. Several

earlier designs had been blocked, including his 1673 design, of
which the 'Great Model' can still be seen in the crypt of the
Cathedral. This is a magnificent design and had it been built it
would have been not only one of the greatest of all baroque masterpieces, but also one of the most technically advanced constructions
of its time. Sadly, the design was too radical, the project was
rejected, and in its place Wren designed the present less innovative
cathedral, so loved by the Prince of Wales.

The defence of modern architecture and its practitioners is a
daring thesis in the present climate in which the architect is blamed
for many of society's ills. I believe that the intervention by the
Prince, however well intended, has delayed rather than advanced
the state of architecture by reinforcing a cynical view of architecture
as a marketing and packaging tool aimed at maximizing profit rather
than improving the quality of the envionment. His attacks have
encouraged cynical developers to obtain planning approval by the
simple procedure of clamping vernacular or classical forms on to
badly designed buildings. This simplistic camouflage successfully
conceals the root cause of the critical state of our built environment.

The exercise of the Royal prerogative should be questioned: for
example, time and again the Prince has singled out individual
architects for criticism. In doing so he is violating the principles of
a constitutional monarchy. Prince Charles should keep his views
at a general rather than personal level. Criticizing individual architects, after all, is not any different from criticizing individual doctors, lawyers, teachers, or even politicians. And it is particularly
regrettable that those he singles out – Professor Colin St John
Wilson, Sir Denys Lasdun, James Stirling and Ahrends Burton &
Koralek – are internationally acknowledged to be among our very
finest architects. They are also among the few British architects
who have avoided the large commercial schemes, which have been
the ruin of so much of our environment. In fact, they were among
the most vocal critics of the quality of British architecture long
before the media jumped on this issue. By singling out these
influential architects the Prince has wasted the opportunity to
involve them in a constructive and non-partisan campaign to
improve architectural standards.

By blaming the architect for the ugliness of the built environment the Prince has misguidedly chosen an easy target. He exonerates the real culprits – the commercial and political institutions that exercise architectural patronage – thereby frustrating the very debate he wishes to encourage and avoiding the political and financial realities. If his reason is that this would overstep acceptable political and economic bounds then he should never have begun his attack, for it leaves the heir to the throne open to serious criticism.

The Prince and his followers have failed to recognize that the poverty of our built environment is part of a much larger and more important crisis. That is, the erosion of our global environment, which is endangering the very world we live in. Had this link been made he might have appreciated that it is not an architectural style which is responsible for the disfigurement, much less the modern movement which has been made an easy scapegoat, but rather the subordination of public value to private greed.

Architecture mirrors society, its civility and its barbarism, the cities and its buildings cannot be better than the sense of social responsibility from which they spring. It is simply not possible for architects to create parks, avenues, squares, fountains or even colonnades without the client's approval, for they are dictated by cost.

Architects, of course, have played their part in the débâcle. Many have been only too willing to concur with their clients, whether developers or public authorities, in the view that their job is to produce a commodity – architecture – which has no bearing on the public at large. While not wishing to excuse the architects who have designed the cheap, shoddy developments, I take the view that blaming them alone obscures the extent to which the large corporations, developers and government are deeply implicated. What long-term interest can be expected if buildings are written off in ten years and annual profitability is the aim of the government, the chairman and shareholders? Ours is an age of business giants and cultural pygmies.

If a quick profit is the only consideration then the most valuable architect is one that can get round the planning system, build faster and use the cheapest materials. So it is hardly surprising that buildings reflect the narrow interests of the market-place rather than the long-term needs of the community.

The British architectural scene since the war has not been notable so much for the poor quality of its architects, as for the lack of spirit of public patronage. There is every reason to believe that all periods produce some good architects and today clients can choose architects from anywhere around the globe. As it is, there is a wealth of British architectural talent which has drawn on and enriched modernism so that it responds tc the needs of the late twentieth century, though one has to go abroad to see many of the best examples: Hong Kong, Germany, France and Japan.

No one blames the artist if a museum has a bad collection, nor the author if a library has a bad selection. So long as there are good artists and good writers the blame must fall on the person whose responsibility it is to select; the same is true of architecture.

Nor should the responsibility of government be underestimated. The Thatcher years have reminded us, if we needed reminding, of the power of government to effect change where there is a will to do so. Certainly this government has the authority to make it plain, through direct patronage, legislation and incentive taxation that the shoddy commercial developments of the past will no longer be tolerated. President Mitterrand has much to teach us in this respect. He has committed himself not to returning to the good old days but, rather, to address the practicalities of promoting higher architectural standards at the end of the twentieth century. In doing so he has strengthened France's position as the leader of western culture.

I believe that the new movements in architecture that sprang up around the turn of this century represent an important turning point in the history of architecture, comparable to that other great watershed, the development of the classical forms of the Renaissance. Like the beautiful buildings of Brunelleschi, Hawksmoor or Borromini the designs of Sullivan, Frank Lloyd Wright, Le Corbusier and Louis Kahn offer a new aesthetic response to the scientific and ethical movement of the times.

Together with these aesthetic principles went certain social commitments. The history of 'Modernism' had as its starting point the disastrous growth of the nineteenth-century city and the spread of slum dwellings. Early efforts in modern design were marked by a concern to develop healthier, greener and more humanitarian environments; English garden cities and new towns reflect this reformist spirit.

From its beginning modern architecture, like its classical fore-runners, has been concerned to incorporate new technology into its designs. Its best buildings have been infused with a spirit of innovation and discovery; they have celebrated the technology with which they were built. The excitement of a technologically adventurous architecture is evident in such modern masterpieces as Paxton's Crystal Palace, Frank Lloyd Wright's Johnson's Wax Factory in Wisconsin and Norman Foster's Hong Kong and Shanghai Bank.

Since the Second World War the pace of change has quickened. One need only look at the world from the perspective of a spacecraft – an impossibility thirty years ago – to realize that a global revolution is taking place. The world has changed from a small number of relatively isolated communities, to a finite industrialized place. Its surface is covered by an infinitely complex information network; it is becoming an artefact, a global village. The miracle of science is all around us. We have two options, either to ignore the tide of progress and to look for support in nostalgic traditions and images of the past, or to face up to the global revolution and to build upon the developments of the past to make society fit for tomorrow.

Architecture will reflect and must benefit from this second industrial revolution. The computer, micro-chip, transputer, bio-technology and solid-state chemistry could lead to an enhanced environment, including more rather than less individual control and few uniform spaces. The best buildings of the future will interact dynamically with people, adapting to the climate, for example, in order to better meet the user's needs. Closer to robots than to temples, these chameleon-like apparitions with their changing surfaces are forcing us once again to rethink the art of architecture. Architecture will no longer be a question of mass and volume but of lightweight structures whose superimposed transparent layers will create form so that architecture will become dematerialized.

In architecture, as elsewhere, it is only through the development of the most modern ideas and techniques that we can solve both functionally and aesthetically the problems that confront us such as shelter for all, overcrowding, traffic, noise, smell and the general erosion of the beautiful qualities of land, sea and air.

It is a delusion to think that returning to a make-believe past can solve this global crisis. In fact, the danger we face is not of being too modern but, rather, of not being modern enough. For the first time we have the knowledge and the means to create a paradise or a rubbish tip on earth. The choice is ours.

Richard Rogers, July 1989

Preface

The Prince of Wales has commanded a forum. It is a forum in which we must speak our minds, and dare to speak for others.

In the current architectural 'debate', however, one voice dominates; that of His Royal Highness. His is the voice of the silent majority, a mandate. And there is no doubt that, for some, the views of the Prince of Wales have become mandatory.

With authority and conviction, the Prince has opened the debate. How, then, is it to proceed? With question and argument. The popular view has been ably articulated from the 'carbuncle' speech (with its litany of complaints against the architectural profession) to the Prince's Ten Commandments, which offer a rule book for the future. We have gone from monologue to catalogue; it is now time for dialogue.

Opposition to the Prince went into voluntary liquidation in the face of sustained and – we are told – overwhelming support for his views. Architects have been caught off-guard by the force of the attack. The Royal *Blitzkrieg* has left a great deal of rubble in its wake. Now we must rebuild, and rebuild not in the shadow of the Throne, but in the light of rationality.

This book is offered neither as an academic work nor as an act of revenge. It is a personal response: the views expressed are mine and are not advanced as being those of the Royal Institute of British Architects, of which I am the 63rd President. I was persuaded to commit some thoughts to paper by those who, like me, believe the critical argument about our built environment has been one-sided. This reply to the Prince of Wales was written in the interest of a continuing and genuine debate; it is also set down as an act of faith on behalf of a profession whose probity and skill has been called into question.

Challenging the beliefs of the Prince of Wales has been as

difficult for architects as for anyone else: we are all locked into notions of reverence for the monarchy, and are aware that counter-arguments are not underwritten by the power and privilege which has given such weight to the Prince's public opinion.

Following the broadcast of the Prince's views in *A Vision of Britain*, the Council of the RIBA held its own debate. In a keynote address Gordon Graham CBE, a past President of the Institute, said:

To HRH The Prince of Wales I would say this: thank you for stimulating the debate. It is good to have it going on. But be fair. Be careful not to abuse your privilege by attacking projects which are *sub judice* awaiting the outcome of a democratic public inquiry.

We admire your capacity to create amusing catchphrases, but maybe they are now becoming less rewarding to your case. This profession longs for the debate to move on from the propaganda phase to more profound discussion. Your recent television programme encourages me to think you want this too. Like Peter Palumbo, I say 'God Bless the Prince of Wales' but question some of his architectural judgements. I would also add three cheers for modern architecture and those architects who will struggle on in the present hostile climate to maintain their creative integrity and strive to meet the objectives of our Royal Charter.

After a long debate, the Council passed the following motion.

This Council welcomes the interest of the Prince of Wales in the built environment; shares his concern for the differing problems of towns, cities and countryside; believes he would accept that the errors of the past were due as much to politicians, planners and developers among others, as to architects; encourages him to acknowledge that there is room for the best in all styles and periods of architecture in creating a high quality of life; and, on behalf of the Institute, will pursue a dialogue in which these matters and the practical realities of building and design can be openly and freely discussed.

The RIBA is emerging from a period of preoccupation with its internal affairs of government and constitution to address matters of national interest which go beyond mere discussion of architectural styles. Housing and the homeless, the planning and development system, transport, safety in buildings, all are now on the agenda. This book was written in the belief that the debate must be taken forward. It is intended to stimulate further discussion rather than stand as an alternative manifesto to the Prince of Wales's vision. It is an emotional, rather than a political, response. On those terms I have set down my subjective views not as measured drawings but as sketches, in an attempt to promote interest not only in what His Royal Highness thinks about architecture, but in the changing social role of architecture itself.

London, May 1989

I
Royalty
at the Crossroads

Nature that fram'd us of four elements,
Warring within our breasts for regiment,
Doth teach us all to have aspiring minds:
Our souls, whose faculties can comprehend
The wondrous Architecture of the world:
And measure every wand'ring planet's course,
Still climbing after knowledge infinite,
And always moving as the restless Spheres,
Will us to wear ourselves and never rest,
Until we reach the ripest fruit of all,
That perfect bliss and sole felicity,
The sweet fruition of an earthly crown.

Christopher Marlowe,
Conquests of Tamburlaine, Prologue

The Prince of Wales's vision of Britain is that of a united kingdom. In it, the citizens are free and prosperous. Bureaucracy rampant has been tamed; the common will finds expression through an active and dynamic democracy. People have a much greater say not only in how their country is governed but in how their neighbourhoods are run. These are the noble and proper aspirations of a monarch, timeless and universal.

The aspirations of a British monarch in the twenty-first century, however, will be timely and specific. The constitutional niche occupied by his ancestors has become inadequate and outdated for His Royal Highness, who has proved himself a modern and unorthodox heir to the throne. Protocol is cumbersome; it intervenes between sovereign and subject. The Prince's eagerness for a better world has caught a popular mood of self-help, and in the restructuring of his public role he has demonstrated by example the effectiveness of individual action. The Prince of Wales is no longer what he does but what he *is*. He has accomplished nothing less than a management buy-out of the monarchy.

His ardent campaigning is applauded as much for the adventuring spirit in which it is conducted as for its intent. He is, in nearly every sense, a modern prince. The royal standards have rallied a moral crusade for change, a crusade in which the Crown will not flinch from challenging the establishment. If the system allows homeless people to sleep huddled in hamlets of damp cardboard, the system is wrong; if the law permits the poisoning of our seas, the law is wrong.

Determined to rewrite his brief, the Prince is a public figure whose time has come. He prefers to cut red tape rather than ribbons. And his articulation of common anxieties has created in him a tribune whose power is peerless and unimpeachable. He might speak only for some of us, but he speaks *to* all of us.

The ideals of a society are enshrined in its architecture. It would be logical for a modern prince to favour a dynamic architecture as part of a world which is progressively more responsive to its people. But the Prince of Wales's visionary Britain is a green and pleasant land in a perpetual golden summer. It is British Summer Time, but everyone has forgotten to put their clocks forward.

'We shape our buildings: thereafter they shape us,' said Sir Winston Churchill in an interview in 1960. By the turn of the century, what shape will we be in? The Prince's preference is for stylistic hierarchy: authoritative classical architecture for the nobs; humble pitched-roof vernacular for the common people. It is a popular preference, one which calls up average denominators of cultural society.

The Prince of Wales's vision is both ordinary and unique. The alienation he feels on behalf of a modern urban population is partly his own, for imagine the isolation which must be the burden of one born to rule. It is an intolerable thought that parts of King Charles's realm might be 'no-go areas'. Yet it is a poignant fact that, for a member of the Royal Family, life is a sequence of 'no-go areas'. On his travels through modern Britain, he is surrounded by two concentric rings of vigilant spectators: the press and the public watching him, and a praetorian guard of security men watching us.

It has always been like this, right from the start. Cecil Beaton's diary records, in December 1948, the Prince's first royal engagement: 'Happily summoned to the Palace to take the first long-awaited photographs of the heir to the throne. Prince Charles was an obedient sitter. He interrupted a long, contented sleep to do my bidding and open his blue eyes to stare long and wonderingly into the camera lens, the beginning of a lifetime in the glare of public duty.'

The Prince's heartfelt concern for those who live in the inner cities is that of the outsider. This is, in one sense, a genuine advantage. A comparative and objective appraisal of our cities rests on the judgement of a man for whom all doors open yet who understands the aspirations of working people; a man, in short, who is both detached and semi-detached. While the Prince has assiduously sought the views of men and women in the street at first hand, much of his education has been on the distance-learning principle, in which his own impressions of a Britain whizzing past his window have been refined by a group of retiring advisers with pensionable views.

There can be few people better placed than the Prince of Wales to give an overview of Britain. From an aeroplane, a helicopter, a limousine, the world divides neatly into town and country. One spoils the other. The built environment looms menacingly, like a Saracen horde advancing into Albion. There is worse news still – an enemy within. Architects, who have lost faith in God and abandoned the people, build pagan temples to themselves and open prisons for the poor.

But there is hope at last: a popular uprising, a Peasants' Revolt, with a royal champion. It is 1981. On television and in the newspapers he sees appalling scenes of rioting. This is not Camelot, it is Babylon – and it is burning. The consumer society's disenfranchized rise up together, black and white, and wreak terrible violence on the built environment and its custodians. The Prince of Wales feels a special kind of helplessness. Although the nation watches the riots and experiences the impotence of the television viewer, the powerlessness felt by the Prince is that of the newscaster for ever condemned to read other people's scripts and wait for his cue. For the heir to the throne, the urban riots presented an unacceptable legacy of disillusionment. With the prospect of a divided nation and the deepening of inner-city squalor, something must be done. People have lost pride in their neighbourhoods and cities because they no longer have a stake in them. They are misunderstood because they are not consulted, and they are not consulted most by architects.

Prince Charles was justly shocked by the televised violence of the inner-city riots. Yet he felt bound, as the people's Prince and future king, to align himself with those community leaders who characterized the mayhem of Brixton, Tottenham, St Paul's and Toxteth as a social-security *Intifada*. The West Bank and Gaza Strip had suddenly come to within a stone's throw of Kensington Palace. What these people were demanding was self-determination. But what of the silent majority, those for whom the Prince now speaks? What were they demanding? Law and order. Communities were blighted by unemployment, scared off the streets, disintegrating. Society was sick and it needed healing. The Prince, bound by the golden chains of constitutional monarchy, could not take too factional a view. The Prince's cause must be both establishment and anti-establishment; it must espouse the virtues of self-help and civic order while offering a fresh populist view. What inner-city neighbourhoods needed, he reasoned, was a new kind of architect with a new vision; not a buildings architect at all, but a people architect, an architect who could build new communities by giving them a reason to work together, a kind of *community* architect . . .

In July 1987 the Prince accepted an invitation from Rod Hackney, president of the Royal Institute of British Architects, to speak at an awards ceremony for *The Times*/RIBA Community Enterprise Scheme. He took the opportunity to speak out on the rival schemes being promoted at the time for the prestigious Spitalfields Market site, and backed the one masterplanned by the neo-classical architect Quinlan Terry. Perplexingly, the Prince said the scheme would both offer the 'unique opportunity for a classical revival' in the East End and stop 'yuppies, for instance, moving into the area'.

He also chose the occasion to warn his audience, rather unnecessarily, that he wanted to 'stir things up, to throw a proverbial royal brick through the inviting plate glass of pompous professional pride and jump feet first into the kind of spaghetti bolognese of red tape which clogs this country from one end to the other'.

The impact of the imagery – the brick thrown through glass, a snapshot from the riots – was undeniable, even if the message was a little unclear. Was he aiming the brick at pomposity or professional pride? Or was he simply unable to resist the alliteration? In any event, the first stone having been cast, my profession has been under siege from an angry mob ever since. We have picked the splinters of glass from our hair and replaced the window again and again, the only sure prescription against vandalism. And anyway, pompous or not, we architects rather cherish our professional pride.

By 1988, however, the Prince's concern for architectural practice had yielded to a new crusade, based almost entirely on style and appearance. If there must be new buildings, let them be vernacular, with pitched roofs and proper windows, or classical, with a reassuring set of semiotic triggers which say, 'This is the way it has always been and this is the way it must always stay.'

Prince Charles's outspoken views on the environment have found a resonance in many people. This is in part due to their reactionary tone, which goes down well with the small shareholder on the Clapham omnibus. We instinctively empathize with the encoded yearning for tradition. As a living part of our Royal Heritage, of course, Prince Charles is well advised to promote a hierarchical view in which there is a place for everyone and everyone is in their place. An Englishman's home is his castle, and we all have an equity stake in the one at Balmoral. Royalty remains the one thing guaranteed not to be done better by the Americans or the Japanese, and we revere it. The monarchy enjoys an unprecedented, if not entirely welcome, openness. The Crown's modern role – carved out by the Glorious Revolution and whittled down by the loss of dominions – is being redefined. The Queen is a figurehead; that's the first thing we learn at school. The pomp is good for tourism and aren't they wonderful ambassadors for Britain abroad? Adapting to a more relaxed view of itself, the Royal Family has reaffirmed our affection with a 'cardigans and corgis' version of life at the top and has made a real effort to be effortlessly real. The Royal Family invited television over for Christmas and it stayed all year; now it is too late to raise the drawbridge. In the popular press, royalty and soap stars make the most readable copy. A national predilection for vicarious living and unashamed prurience has helped shape the relationship between Charles and 'the nation'.

For the architectural profession, that relationship took a dramatic turn in 1985, when an alleged confession of Charles's fears for a 'divided Britain' hit the headlines. The story was sourced by journalists to Rod Hackney, by now a royal confidant and architectural adviser. Architecture was dragged on to the front page like a recalcitrant nightclubber, shielding its face from the flash. Hackney was to weather the storm of outrage from within his own profession at what appeared to be a gross infringement of confidentiality and was returned in triumph as the president-elect of the RIBA in 1986 on a wave of popular support for both him and the man he intimately referred to as 'HRH'.

After years of struggling inside the straitjacket of a public image which portrayed him as the perpetual undergraduate with funny friends and a penchant for excruciating wisecracks, the Prince has found a serious mission. Every loyal subject will wish him greater understanding of the task ahead. The tabloids' Clown Prince had hung up his red nose for good and was ready to do battle; Prince Hal transformed to Agincourt's Henry – 'Reply not to me with a fool-born jest, presume not that I am the thing I was. For God doth know, so shall the world perceive, that I have turned away my former self.' Goodbye, Neddy Seagoon; hello, Laurens van der Post.

When, in 1987, the Prince assembled a small group of newspaper editors for an off-the-record lunch (NB: There's no such thing as an off-the-record lunch), he complained that the cheap end of the press would not take him seriously, that his life with Diana was being treated as a soap opera. The implication was that this was somehow a diminution of his place in the hearts of his people.

This is a misreading. It is true that royalty is a popular soap, but it always has been. Victorian society hummed with gossip about the Prince of Wales, Georgian society was titillated by scandal about the Prince Regent (was Mary Ann Nash, wife of the royal architectural adviser, really a royal mistress?). It's a fair bet that even Boudicca had a few 'sexy secrets'. Royals, like soap stars, age and change with us. I have always felt a certain affection for the Prince of Wales because we are the same age – I am three weeks younger. We have, as a nation, watched the family grow older as we have grown older. The Royal Family is *there* to be gazed at, after all. As we are their people, so they are ours. There is as much concern over Charles and Diana's marriage as there is over Charlene and Scott's, as much straight talking about Fergie and Beatrice as there was about Mary and Annie (Come back, Mary. Albert Square needs you). While the nation's unbridled affection for the Queen Mother grows with every passing year, we do not much like the prospect of an old king's coronation. Most of us want the Prince of Wales to feel he has a useful role to play. He must be encouraged to speak out, for his unique position in society allows him to champion causes and further the aims of environmental groups with a force unparalleled outside party politics. He has a role model in his sister, who modulated from a haughty Princess Anne to a massively popular Princess Royal and found new purpose in her championing of the Save the Children Fund.

When the Prince of Wales called for a vote of confidence in his public crusade, he got it by a landslide. I suggest, however, that what Charles has secured is not a mandate from the people to bash architects but *carte blanche* to bash whomever he wishes in the interests of a more proactive monarchy. How many 'don't knows' are there among the silent majority? And for those who have no fixed ideas about classical architecture or pitched roofs, which is the more romantic view – that of the unfathomably eclectic architect or that of the heir to the throne for whom life begins at forty?

Well, two cheers for the Prince of Wales. He has done more than anyone in the last decade to popularize the debate about architecture. But his intervention has changed – in a sense, obliterated – the debate. It is now reduced to a kind of civil war in which the Royalists outnumber the Republicans five to one. Over the years, the Prince has spoken out against large-scale redevelopment generally, and against certain architectural schemes specifically. His opinions are seen to carry the weight of popular opinion and are taken very seriously indeed by architects' clients and local authority planners; his intervention has led effectively to the sacking of some architects from important and worthwhile projects. As soon as the Prince enters the debate, considered reflection gives way to hasty genuflection. The Prince has accepted the brief for a people's tribune at a national level. Opinion polls tell us that his assumption of implicit support from a majority of people is justified. But is the 'country' really cheering him on as a spokesman for the people or as an advocate for the Government? As long as the Prince concentrates on architectural style and professional arrogance, and keeps out of the wider political debate on a 'nation divided', he serves the interests of Downing Street.

Mrs Thatcher is said to have been furious when the alleged views of the future king exploded in the press and the House of Commons while she was away in Washington. The Queen, too, was embarrassed. Here was the heir to the throne publicly articulating the dangerous notion that the realm was divided. This helped neither the Crown nor the Government.

Architecture as a profession, however, was fair game. Leading lights in the Conservative Government have made no secret of their desire to do for the professions what they have done for the trade unions. That is, do for them. All the professions are currently under pressure to restructure along the lines of the Continental and American models, in which the professions are firmly part of the bourgeois culture and shorn of those lingering fuddy-duddy ideas of a wider social responsibility.

The Prince of Wales has chosen largely to ignore the major economic forces which are shaping 'Enterprise Britain'. It is, by inference, all right for developers to assemble massive city-centre sites or for clients to demand major new office schemes. The argument begins and ends with the design. Prince Charles's sorties into London's Docklands are instructive in this regard. On seeing Cesar Pelli's 800-foot central tower for the £4 billion Canary Wharf scheme, a project which envisages London as the financial capital of the world, he asked, 'Why does it have to be so big?' On visiting the Docklands Design Museum, a high-tech building with high-tech neighbours, he asked, 'Why doesn't it have a pitched roof?'

The Prince has shown enormous courage in speaking out on the built environment. I would argue, though, that his comments have been well aimed but misguided. He has gathered around him advisers who are passionate, highly motivated and unanimous. it must be incredibly difficult for the Prince to make value judgements on what he sees around him. What kind of culture shock must it have been for him when he saw his first slum? He relies on the right signals filtering through a permanent forcefield of security and privilege wherever he goes.

In his provocative broadcast to the nation in 1988, called *A Vision of Britain*, we see him gazing out of the window as William Blake's England rolls majestically past. He is apparently alone on an antique train. This is mouthwateringly real: 'Lifestyles of the Rich and Famous'. The antique train is, of course, being pulled by a modern engine of the sort that ferries InterCity passengers across the country, but that is not seen from the panelled interior. The Prince gives us his view of the urban landscape: there is not a building in sight.

Just how sanitized an experience the royal Odyssey can be – both metaphorically and literally – is open to speculation. Just as Charles's father was a prince before him, so my father was an architect before me. I remember as a child the Queen Mother coming to open one of my father's buildings, a modest pitch-roofed brick-clad nurses' home in Grantham, where we lived (I even used to buy my sweets from *that* corner shop). Everyone from the chairman of Rotary downwards lined up. My mother was terribly upset because my father wasn't presented, but although he wasn't invited to the opening, he was instructed at the last minute to upgrade the WC suite, 'just in case' the Queen Mum was taken short. *Plus ça change* . . .

First stop on the royal Odyssey – perhaps it should be Iliad, as Charles has yet to enter Troy – is Skipton, a modest northern town expressive of the dilemmas facing post-industrial Britain. The

Prince quite rightly praises some new low-rise housing. It is well built and nicely detailed. The city fathers are praised for their efforts to preserve the character of the town. What this means in demonstrable terms is the preservation of nineteenth-century terraced housing and a new shopping arcade. The housing looks better the further away you are; it is built from local materials and is comfortingly familiar in its form.

Despite the welcome improvements, however, it remains back-to-back housing built for the working class, with poor daylighting. What on earth has it got to do with the 1980s? Do we really want to keep our housing the way it was 100 years ago? The phoney philosophy of traditionalism is better expressed in the town's new shopping centre – a fantasy Victorian repro affair which has a glazed roof over the original street. This is Hovis-commercial architecture, refining a culture that never existed in the first place. Victorian shopping was never like this. Ironwork shows the detailing of railway stations and would never have been used in conjunction with granite on so small a scale. Fake London Georgian doors have been grafted on. It is a deceitful Disneyland for our children to inherit in which history has been rewritten by the packaging of experiences. Real architecture is real history, not repro. Skipton's Victorian market would have witnessed privation, exploitation, poverty and disease, not a bored shop assistant listening to Radio Two in Mr Humbug's Olde Sweete Shoppe.

I was in Leeds recently. The cab driver – all the antique trains had been taken – didn't seem to share the Prince's misgivings about comprehensive redevelopment. 'Look!' he said, pointing at the buildings. 'Things are booming. We're finally getting what this city deserves.' Others I spoke to shared his enthusiasm and optimism. In areas of high unemployment and low expectation all over the country, the construction boom is seen as a tangible sign of confidence in the future. I may hate the fake Victoriana of a shopping arcade, the Prince may hate the vast bulk of a new office block, but then we both have our axes to grind. For the vast majority of people, I submit, regeneration is welcomed rather than feared. Many of the buildings being pulled down now are not Victorian or Georgian masterpieces but office and industrial buildings of the 1960s which have outlived their usefulness. Is it necessarily so bad that our cities are constantly reforming themselves, refitting the urban landscape to match changing circumstances? The buildings replacing 1960s blocks in the middle of cities now are not eternal, any more than their predecessors were. They will last as long as they are viable – longer, if the architecture commends itself to the public – and will fall when their time is up. They are not part of some sinister architectural Thousand-Year Reich.

Indeed, in both Leeds and Cardiff, Prince Charles expresses fondness for buildings I regard as utterly totalitarian in conception. His fear is that the grand civic buildings of Victoria and Edward will be marginalized, 'snubbed' by new development. Good. If they are to be seen as part of our heritage, they should be pensioned off. They have nothing to do with a modern, growing city. These vast civic buildings must have towered over the people who built them in a way almost impossible to comprehend now. For they were not ordinary office buildings in which ordinary people would work. They glorified the hierarchy of a paternalistic world. These municipal giants spoke of empire. What consultation was there before they were built? If anything was non-contextual, surely it was these monumental edifices erected as part of a national preoccupation with self-importance and dignity and the worst kind of civic jingoism. The people who built them were neglected. They had no say. They were relegated to cheap and cheerless housing. Why do we strive to commemorate this?

In Cardiff, a massive programme of change is planned for the city, its docks and its bay. The Prince makes an oft-repeated plea for conservation. Of what? Crumbling houses? An urban wasteland? A bay polluted to a poisonous level? The Prince fears that the fine old listed wharf buildings will tumble in the path of progress. This will be very difficult and, furthermore, make little sense to the developers. In maritime and docklands schemes throughout the country developers are not only charged by national regulations and local authority plans with preserving the listed buildings; they are also, with increasing accord, exploiting the loss-leading possibilities a tastefully refurbished Victorian warehouse can bring to schemes which succeed or fail on the numbers of users they can

attract. The conservation battle has been fought and won, internationally.

In 1975, I was involved in a rather self-congratulatory event
hosted jointly by the RIBA and the Civic Trust to mark European
Architectural Heritage Year. It was clear that conservationists had
finally captured the centre ground, that there was now a climate
of opinion which said no buildings of quality should be pulled
down at all. If someone wanted something out of the way, they'd
have to produce compelling reasons to a hostile public, or they'd
have to send in the bulldozers under cover of darkness. Not that
both haven't happened in the last two decades, and the vigilant
conservationist will say that listing didn't prevent the wanton
destruction of Sir John Fetherstonhaugh's seminal Smogthorpe
Mill, which only needed £6 million to be restored. What a missed
opportunity! Even now we might have been able to stroll past the
Spinning Jenny Coffee House and Snack Bar.

Please don't misunderstand me. I love old buildings; old churches especially. From my flat in London I look past Hawksmoor's
Bloomsbury church across town to Centrepoint: two of my favourite
London buildings. It would break my heart to see that church
disappear, and I understand the great sentiment which attaches to
certain old buildings. But for every handful of lovely buildings
which has disappeared, a wheelbarrowload has been listed. The
Department of the Environment had, by the end of 1988, listed
no fewer than 426,846 buildings in England alone. There are more
than 35,500 in Scotland, another 11,500 in Wales and 7,500 in
Northern Ireland. When current updating of the DoE's list is
complete, there will be more than 500,000 listed buildings. It
means that, at the end of the latest listing harvest, more than 2 per
cent of the national building stock will be listed: one building in
every fifty.

Next stop on the royal *Vision of Britain* Orient Express is Birmingham, where proposals are forging ahead for a new Convention
Centre ('an unmitigated disaster' – HRH the Prince of Wales). He
is depressed and 'terribly demoralized' because it is turning its
back on Birmingham's Victorian past. But our backs *are* turned;
the world has spun on. He is concerned that the canals are not

made more of, that they are relegated to being backwaters. But they *are* backwaters; canals were utilitarian transport systems, not twee amenity areas. If we are able to find a new use for obsolete relics of the past, fine. But let us not pretend that we are engaged in restoration: it is recycling. (The Bull Ring, by the way, is to go, with the blessing of practically every architect in the country. It really is a horrible mess.)

But the whole point of demolition is to make way for something new, and something better, for the future. One enduring image from the Prince's television programme is that of the future king of England struggling with a ball and chain in a vain attempt to demolish a car park. The stubborn concrete decks had to stand in for residential blocks: the royal voiceover was condemning the 'sad legacy of 1960s housing' as the weight came down. I was consumed with envy: a personal train, a personal helicopter, a personal boat and now the boyhood ambition of smashing something up with a wrecking machine unfolding before my eyes.

Condemning great swathes of his realm is one thing, but promoting a twenty-first-century alternative is another. We cannot simply build cottages everywhere to live in and Temples of Diana everywhere to work in. If Charles's views were as uncompromisingly modern as they are traditionalist, the measure of support, I suggest, would have been equal. If it had been his father who had called for a rerun of the Renaissance and the Prince of Wales who had said, 'It would be a pity if regeneration created eighteenth-century cities in the twenty-first century' (instead of the other way round) I am sure the Prince would not have lacked support. Architecture has been chosen as the forum in which the heir to the throne is arguing for nothing less than the rewriting of the monarch's role in a parliamentary democracy, as a supra-political backstop. The challenge is to find a positive rather than a negative message, to lead rather than to obstruct.

At the moment, the Prince is a rebel without a Court. Who knows what modifications might be made to his views? They have already gone from black and white to sepia. It is not a vision of Britain we need, but a Britain of vision. Anyone can have a vision and, as anyone can also have a television, they can have someone else's vision instead if they wish. We need a national will to change things for the better, and the belief that that is achievable. And we need to spend some serious money. It is possible to learn the lessons of the past without re-creating it; a living heritage museum is a nice place to visit but none of us would want to live there. Perhaps if the Prince took less advice from his own unofficial 1930s Society (a typical member, one suspects, would submit his bill in guineas and list his telephone number as TERminus 5972) and took rather more from the 1990s Society, we might all find it easier to catch up on our homework and prepare for the third millennium.

2
The Great Fire
of London

The horror expressed by the Prince of Wales and others at what has happened to Britain is at its most poignant when applied to London. It is not mass hysteria exactly; it is more a kind of Rip van Winkle syndrome.

The cacophony of new construction issuing from building sites all over the capital – the banging, drilling, shouting and swearing rising to a shriek above the constant blare of Capital Radio – has woken many from a long slumber. They blink and gasp at London transformed, London transforming even as they watch. What has happened to the London of Canaletto and Wordsworth? Earth has not anything to show more foul than the view from Westminster Bridge, and dull of soul have we indeed become if this is how we live. Romantics rub their eyes and try to persuade themselves that it is all a dream, a nasty nightmare from which they will emerge to find John Nash, rather than Richard Rogers, preparing his latest masterplan.

The recent regeneration of London has coincided with a millennial concentration of concern about the way our capital city looks. The same thing happened exactly 100 years ago: a rash of polemical fantasies appeared, speculating on what life would be like at the end of the twentieth century. Just as our own contemporary soothsayers are influenced by the political fashion of the times, so were they. The utopian fantasies of the 1880s and 1890s were largely founded on an innocent Marxism and postulated an automated and egalitarian world in which the people worked less and owned more. The prognoses offered today spring from the pragmatism of the late twentieth century, an era in which the political leader of the Soviet Union tours Europe trying to drum up business with the tantalizing prospect of millions of consumers queuing up to watch *The Benny Hill Show* and shop at Marks and Spencer.

Just over 100 years ago, in 1888, the idea of a machine-age utopia found its popular apotheosis in Edward Bellamy's *Looking Backward*. In it, the hero awakes in Boston in the year 2000: America has evolved into a ruthlessly bureaucratic socialist state. Right prediction, wrong continent. Bellamy's proto-Stalinism divides citizens' lives into four stages – compulsory education to the age of twenty-one, three years' community service, vocational work to forty-five, retirement. Mass production, high technology and a vast civil service conspired in a highly systematic future world.

The book sold by the ton, and it outraged William Morris. An alternative vision of Britain was published by Morris a few years later, in 1891. Called *News from Nowhere*, it is a romance, pure and simple. The hero travels even further than Bellamy's, into twenty-first-century London, where the inhabitants are smartly but casually dressed and live lives of tranquillized equilibrium. Unlike Bellamy's protagonist, Morris's narrator wakes up at the *end* of the book. It has all been a dream! Some of us are still having the same dream 100 years later. Morris's utopian vision is anti-bureaucratic, idyllic and contrasts deliberately with Bellamy's cheerless, beerless Metropolis. This is, rather, Metroland. Hammersmith Broadway is 'wide sunny meadows and garden-like tillage'. The Houses of Parliament are now used as a vast silo for manure. Piccadilly is a rural market. Modernity is alien. The houses and the clothes are fourteenth century. It is as if we are seeing a mythical past risen from the ashes of the future. Society is not moulded by appropriate technology but woven together by an Arts and Crafts ideology.

We came presently into a large open space, sloping somewhat toward the south, the sunny site of which had been taken advantage of for planting an orchard, mainly, as I could see, of apricot trees, in the midst of which was a pretty gay little structure of wood, painted and gilded, that looked like a refreshment stall . . .

Morris's hero asks 'what the stately building is on our left just showing at the end of that grove of plane trees?' He is told,

Ah, that is an old building built before the middle of the twentieth century and as you see, in a queer fantastic style not over beautiful; but there are some fine things inside it, too, mostly pictures, some very old. It is called the National Gallery.

In Morris's utopia, the class revolution means the triumph of the bourgeoisie. Work is a spree, a joy. He comes upon a gang of road-menders. Capital Radio has not been invented.

There were about a dozen of them, strong young men, looking much like a boating party at Oxford . . . their outer raiment lay on the roadside in an orderly pile . . . I could see the gleam of gold and silk embroidery on it . . . beside them lay a good big basket that had hints about it of cold pie and wine . . . They are in luck today: it's right down good sport trying how much pick-work one can get into an hour . . .

Interestingly, although most of Morris's London is now sparsely populated, the City itself is densely packed. The slums of east London have been cleared and the inhabitants have taken over the 'gambling booths' of the Square Mile, where they have grown used to living at high density. Docklands is largely ignored, since 'we have long ago dropped the pretension to be the market of the world.' But

what with the beasts and the men, and the scattered red-tiled roofs and the big hayricks, it does not make a bad holiday to get a quiet pony and ride about there on a sunny afternoon. There is a place called Canning's Town and further out, Silvertown, where the pleasant meadows are at their pleasantest.

In twenty-first-century Britain, everyone dresses up, uses lead-glazed crockery and can identify a good Bordeaux blindfolded. Interior decoration is very . . . well, very *William Morris* really.

Back in the real world of London 1990, we are older and wiser. Or are we? Since the Prince of Wales took centre stage in the great debate, there has been a flurry of interest in London and its future. Are we going somewhere or nowhere?

The Prince and his supporters want, like Morris, to plough up the East End and put in its place a leafy Elysium dotted with cottages, each with its own garden. The formula, however, is not a kind of upmarket communism, but the hard-nosed pragmatism of the private sector. We see the Prince at Bow, touring a new estate which has been built under a public-sector/developer deal. The houses have gardens and have themselves been executed in the familiar, late-1980s, good-investment vernacular. The design is shallow, the detailing appalling: windows are too large and angled to run parallel with the pitch of the roof. The houses conform, however, to the two main strictures of Ideal Home crusaders. They have brickwork and a tiled, pitched roof. Change the specification to concrete and profiled steel, though, and you're on to a loser, no matter how attractive they may look with landscaping and planting. The current obsession with playing it safe is leading us all up a garden path to a capital city full of ghosts and echoes.

The past has gone. We should let it go, but we should also let it stay. Old buildings of quality deserve our guardianship for they inspire us. They inspire us with a sense of continuity and of space shaped by time in a dynamic impulse from cave daubings to computer-controlled intelligent buildings. A nineteenth-century Gothic revival town hall proudly survives amid a wash of functional office blocks conceived a century later; its survival does not tell us that this architectural style marks the summit of our ascent to civilization. It is a building of its time, as Norman Foster's Hong Kong and Shanghai Bank building is of its time. Both will appear quaint 100 years from now. Are we really saying that a Georgian town house is the apex of urban living? We might just as well argue for a return to the horse and cart. Each step in the development of architecture has been a step forward; retracing our steps would be taking a road to nowhere. Architecture is a dynamic art and must evolve to survive in any meaningful way; decorating our cities with the reproduction furniture of neo-classicism is as absurd as repainting a Constable landscape with a Vauxhall Cavalier in the foreground.

New battles are being fought on old battlefields. London is traditionally a city of squares, both in its layout and in the complexion of its City Corporation.

It was a scheme for the most famous square of all which, in 1984, drew the Prince of Wales into architectural controversy with his Hampton Court speech at the RIBA's 150th anniversary. His intervention, just one week before the Secretary of State for the

Environment, Patrick Jenkin, received the public inquiry inspector's report, was a major factor in persuading the dithering trustees of the National Gallery to tear up the scheme by architect Ahrends Burton and Koralek.

In the same speech the Prince dealt a similarly mortal blow to Peter Palumbo's plan to build a beautiful Mies van der Rohe tower as part of a grand scheme to create a new Mansion House Square. Subsequently, the Prince has forced the resignation of Richard Rogers from the Paternoster Square project. Nobody can say that his influence has been slight. His avowed wish to shatter the windows of the architectural profession and jump feet first into controversy has been carried out relentlessly. His is the single most powerful voice in the architectural forum today, and it is swelled by a mighty chorus.

To whom is he accountable? Everyone or no one? Both. His political position is neutral because it is circumspect: he is for self-help, for enterprise, for tradition. As the future king, his destiny is to rule, if not to command, and the head of a constitutional monarchy in the twenty-first century will clearly need demonstrable public support. The Prince of Wales is surfing into the 1990s on a high tide of public opinion. But the mandate for his views on architecture was deduced before it was proven. The banner under which the Prince has rallied his support is that of an armchair crusade; his views are suitable for family viewing. His vision of London is one in which new buildings, if not proscribed, are made either to cringe and cower out of sight or else to dress in ridiculous, old-fashioned costumes for an historical drama now in its 200th successful year. He is the common man, the man in the saloon bar who likes a good strong tune and believes they don't write them like that anymore. His views are simultaneously innocuous and destructive.

His articulation of concern over our urban landscape began in the salubrious setting of Sir Christopher Wren's Hampton Court in 1984. We join him at the segue which, improbably, links 'community architecture' and the Palumbo plan for Mansion House Square:

On that note I can't help thinking how much more worthwhile it would be if a community approach could have been used in the Mansion House Square project. It would be a tragedy if the character and skyline of our capital city were to be further ruined and St Paul's dwarfed by yet another giant glass stump, better suited to downtown Chicago than the City of London. It is hard to imagine that London before the last war must have had one of the most beautiful skylines of any great city, if those who recall it are to be believed. Those who do say that the affinity between buildings and the earth, in spite of the city's immense size, was so close and organic that the houses looked almost as though they had grown out of the earth and had not been imposed upon it – grown moreover, in such a way that as few trees as possible were thrust out of the way . . . What, then, are we doing to our capital city now? What have we done to it since the bombing during the war? What are we shortly going to do to one of its most famous areas – Trafalgar Square? Instead of designing an extension to the elegant façade of the National Gallery which complements it and continues the concept of columns and domes, it looks as if we may be presented with a kind of vast municipal fire station, complete with the sort of tower that contains the siren. I would understand better this type of high-tech approach if you demolished the whole of Trafalgar Square and started again with a single architect responsible for the entire layout, but what is proposed is like a monstrous carbuncle on the face of a much loved and elegant friend. Apart from anything else, it defeats me why anyone wishing to display the early Renaissance pictures belonging to the gallery should do so in a new gallery so manifestly at odds with the whole spirit of that age of astonishing proportion. Why can't we have those curves and arches that express feeling in design? What is wrong with them? Why has everything got to be vertical, straight, unbending, only at right angles – and functional? As if the National Gallery extension wasn't enough they are now apparently planning to redevelop the large, oval-bellied nineteenth-century building, known as the Grand Hotel, which stands on the south west corner of Trafalgar Square and which was saved from demolition in 1974 after a campaign to rescue it. As with the National Gallery, I believe, the plan is to put this redevelopment out to competition, in which case we can only criticize the judges and not the architects, for I suspect there will be some entries representative of the present-day school of romantic pragmatism, which could at least provide an alternative. Goethe once said, 'There is nothing more dreadful than imagination without taste.'

As it turned out, there was rather more taste than imagination involved in the battle for Trafalgar Square. The fiasco that was the National Gallery competition began in 1981, with the announcement by Michael Heseltine, then Environment Secretary, that a two-stage developer/architect competition would be held. It was hobbled from the start by two factors: one was that instead of architectural assessors, the Government – through the executive arm of the Property Services Agency – appointed advisers, who were thus separated from the client, the gallery's own board of trustees; the other critical factor was the brief itself, which was a shotgun marriage of culture and commerce.

The deal was this: the Government would give the site (a bomb site turned car park) to the winning developer on a 125–year lease at a peppercorn rent in exchange for the rent-free leaseback of a gallery extension above. There would be 34,000 square feet of gallery space, and 66,000 square feet of office space with an annual rental value assessed in 1981 at £1 million. Today, that office space is worth around £4.3 million; a 6.6 per cent yield gives a capital value of £65 million.

Prime commercial office space and early Renaissance paintings – these priorities are not easy to juggle. Nevertheless, there were seventy-nine entries, whittled down to a short list of seven second-stage schemes by May 1982. The short-listed schemes went on display at the gallery, and the public were invited to vote for their favourite. Up to 1,500 people a day visited the exhibition. I went, and voted for the Richard Rogers scheme, which was by far the most exciting and celebratory, with its Dan Dare and the Mekons tower, and the only one really to extend the brief to include the user client – the visitor to Trafalgar Square as well as the National Gallery. It was not simply an extension; it created a new boulevard and a pedestrian subway between Trafalgar Square and Leicester Square. It would have liberated the whole area.

Another lunch-time visitor to the exhibition was Owen Luder, then president of the RIBA. His support for the Rogers scheme was unequivocal and public; conversational remarks made within earshot of a journalist from *The Times* surfaced the following day, transformed into a strident pre-emptive judgement. 'I hope they have the courage to choose that one,' Mr Luder said. 'That is the work of a man who has said, "That is what I think the answer is and sod you." The others have all been overwhelmed by the site.'

The jury was, so to speak, directed to ignore the remarks. But by now nobody was quite sure how much weight public comment carried. By October 1982, the assessors had asked three of the seven short-listed practices – Ahrends Burton and Koralek, Arup Associates and Skidmore Owings and Merrill – to take part in an unscheduled play-off. All three were to modify their schemes, from which a winner was to be chosen. People were beginning to ask why a competition had been held in the first place, when the unlucky seventy-two entrants from the original batch had been given no opportunity to redesign as the brief modulated. An overall winner was promised by the competition organizers in September, then November. The 'winner' was announced just before Christmas as part of a desk-clearing spate of decisions by the departing Environment Secretary, Michael Heseltine. ABK was announced as the winning architectural practice, but the brief was *still* being haggled over. Tension between the National Gallery trustees and the panel of advisers was palpable, and there was understandable dissatisfaction among the other competitors. What had started as a design competition had changed into a selection process for the architect, and the first major public debate about architecture since the Festival of Britain had become a venomous row over the way the competition had been run.

The Prince of Wales's interest was by now keen, though discreet. While ABK were back at the drawing board, mischievous schemes abounded, including an impressive offering from architect and critic Roderick Gradidge, who dismissed the need for the 'absurdly unnatural' combination of offices and gallery extension by adding height and new wings to the existing gallery and developing the car park site next door for offices alone. The impatience for a real scheme, however, was growing and there was further disappointment in July 1983. ABK's fourth design was due to go on public display. Instead, the trustees again sent the architects back to make additional 'refinements'. Meanwhile, the country had its third Environment Secretary of the year – Patrick Jenkin had replaced Tom King. The amended, revised, torn-up and started-again, refined and improved ABK scheme was finally approved by the trustees in December 1983. It was instantly attacked by Westminster City Council's planning committee as 'unacceptable in design terms ... insipid and timid ... just another office block with expensive cladding'.

The public inquiry opened in April 1984, just as the Prince of Wales was starting to prepare his speech. The inspector's report was received by Jenkin a week after the Prince delivered his *coup de grâce*. Opposition at the inquiry was characterized more by distaste for the competition concept of mixing commerce and art than by distaste for ABK's scheme. Displaying the kind of client loyalty which ABK had enjoyed throughout the saga, the trustees gave warning that they might still call for the latest scheme to be stopped, pending tests on a mock-up of part of it. The developer, Trafalgar House, said it would pull out unless planning permission was granted by the end of September. They never made it: at the beginning of September Jenkin overruled the inquiry recommendation – which was approval for the ABK scheme – and turned it down.

The inquiry inspector, David Woolley, QC, had argued that refusal could jeopardize redevelopment on the site. The official DoE letter to ABK and the developers took note of the inspector's comments but ruled that the glazed tower – added to the scheme on the insistence of gallery trustees – would be 'alien to the character of existing buildings in the vicinity and would constitute an unwelcome intrusion into Trafalgar Square. In view of the serious objections to the proposed tower, the only issue on which the objectors were to any extent united, the Secretary of State sees no alternative but to refuse both planning permission and listed building consent.'

For nearly three years, the architects had doggedly followed the constantly changing brief with patience and skill; the developers had spent £1 million on the exercise. By the time the Prince of Wales entered the debate so unequivocally, the competition system which had generated the beleaguered design had been entirely discredited.

A bad brief, conflicting signals from a factionalized client group and years of indecision and inactivity on the site itself furnished an ideal opportunity for censure from the Prince. The architects, however, bore the brunt. Stigmatized by the strident invective, ABK were reviled as the authors of a scheme for which they had become the executors.

The National Gallery extension had turned into a tragic embarrassment for both the trustees and the government. After the Prince's enthusiastic denunciation, it had become easier to find a scapegoat – the architects' 'fire station' tower – and call the whole thing off.

An apocryphal tale that the Prince had mistaken ABK's scheme for the earlier one by Richard Rogers has been circulating ever since the débâcle. Certainly, the futurist design of Rogers's scheme was far less 'contextual' than ABK's and could more readily be assumed to have outraged conservative sensibilities.

However ill-briefed the Prince had been, the effect of his speech was a practical demonstration of the power of royal intervention.

There had been no classical scheme among the original seven short-listed schemes. The climate had changed considerably in the wake of the royal speech, though, and when in April 1985 the trustees announced that a new wing would be paid for by the Sainsbury brothers, ABK were told they would not be designing it. Lord Annan, chairman of the trustees, said, 'This time we hope we will get a building that is worthy of Trafalgar Square and especially worthy and sympathetic to Wilkins's building. It must harmonize with it.'

With admirable self-restraint and generosity of spirit, Peter Ahrends welcomed the 'benefit to the gallery' of the Sainsburys' gift. It would, of course, have been so much easier if a donation had been secured four years earlier, when one of the Sainsburys was on the board of trustees. The inclusion of speculative office space in the scheme could have been avoided in the brief. Although ABK had been treated with 'great courtesy' by the trustees, it had been obvious since the three-scheme short-list that they had favoured the design by Skidmore Owings and Merrill. As top-level discussions had ground on throughout the fiasco, the architects had never been invited to meetings and had only heard officially that they were to be dropped the day before the news appeared in the national press.

Ahrends said, 'Not being present at the meetings registers what society feels about architects. Having won the competition on the basis of drawings, it is at one level quite shocking that the architects should not be present at these discussions.'

The portfolios of thirty architectural practices were seen by the trustees during the summer of 1985. It was a sign of the times that of the six practices short-listed in October two were American. In January 1986 the winner was announced: Robert Venturi, an eminent American architect and Yale professor, of Venturi Rauch and Scott-Brown. 'The building will grow out of the context of the main building by means of harmony and analogy,' he promised. Meanwhile, Skidmore Owings and Merrill, runners-up to ABK in the original competition, were busy planning Canary Wharf.

The selection of Venturi was loaded with significance. His *Complexity and Contradiction in Architecture* is one of the century's most important architectural treatises, and the antidote to a Miesian modernism. By the time Venturi was appointed, the Mies tower for Mansion House Square had been abandoned after a public inquiry held in the shadow of the Prince's 'glass stump' remark.

Venturi was a post-modern heavyweight and a primary agent in the move away from an uncompromisingly modern style. Mies's famous dictum, 'Less is more', had been challenged by Venturi's urbane observation that 'Less is a bore.' He was the perfect architect for a landmark building in a capital city whose evolution was increasingly influenced by a popular prince. The design itself is a study in invisible architecture. The corner of the new building nearest to the gallery is dense with pilasters replicated from the main building and a copycat classical cornice. The unbridled classicism is then gradually faded out as the building turns away from the main gallery, in a gentle decoding which ends in a more or less blank wall. It is skilful, deferential and anodyne. It is, in other words, exactly what the Prince wants.

The grim saga of the National Gallery extension is now at an end, but its repercussions are evident. The mishandling of the competition gave the Prince an ideal opportunity to step into the debate and launch his public crusade. That opportunity should never have arisen: the gallery extension should have been built, or under way, by the time he made his Hampton Court speech.

The fact that he was able so decisively to influence the final appearance of a major building in a place of such great national pride had a direct influence on one of the National Gallery's neighbours, the Victorian block known as Grand Buildings. The result of an architectural competition held by developers Land Securities was a winning entry by Sidell Gibson.

The declared aim of this solution was to disturb Trafalgar Square as little as possible. The existing, outdated and inefficient Victorian corner block was demolished to make way for a new building on the same site which will look eerily similar. Behind the façade is a complex of modern offices designed for practical use well into the twenty-first century. What we see on the outside, however, is something close to a copy of the original, with old-fashioned fenestration and a ground-level arcade. Architecture here serves a kind of civic deference to the past; the influence of the twentieth century on the site of buildings clustered around Trafalgar Square has been hidden from view. This formula, thanks in large part to the Prince of Wales, has become the formula for 'change'.

And change there must be: between now and the end of the century, it is anticipated that a third of the floorspace in the City will be redeveloped to accommodate the evolving demands of the financial sector. The pre-eminence of the City as a world money centre has started a new Fire of London, an invisible and electronic conflagration whose effect is to create rather than destroy the character of London. The new elixir of prosperity is international finance, traded screen-to-screen across continents in seconds.

Electronic dealing is a modern phenomenon. The neophobia shown by those who dread modernization is as anachronistic as the buildings in the City – some of them a mere twenty years old – which themselves are hopelessly out of date. The importance of international finance to the British economy is reflected in the net overseas earnings of UK financial institutions. In 1976, the total was £3,745 million; in 1986, £9,375 million.

Francis Duffy and Alex Henney's book *The Changing City* is both timely (1989) and well informed (one author is an architect, the other an economist). In it, they call for a new popular debate on urban planning, one in which everyone has a voice.

It is up to those who love London and to those who are amateurs of architecture to ensure that London's beauty is enhanced. Comparison with another art form may make our point more clearly. At the end of the nineteenth century England, in musical terms, was a desert – *'Das Land ohne Musik'*. At that time England's architecture (in its domestic manifestations at least) was enormously admired abroad, not least in Germany.

By the middle of this century, and even more obviously in later decades, as a result of continuous improvement in musical education and an enormous growth in popular musical awareness, London has become one of the world's great musical capitals. During the same period the number of amateurs of architecture has not increased to anything like the same degree. English architectural awareness is now primitive in comparison to English musical taste.

Shaping our cities for tomorrow is the primary task both for those who live in them and those who own them. But how can we have a balanced debate when it is the experts who hold the information and the amateurs who hold the floor? The argument over architecture has broadened considerably in the wake of the Prince's comments; it is now a mile wide and an inch deep. It goes, in truth, no deeper than affinity or otherwise with the Prince's view. What should be an intense argument has become mere demarcation. The Prince's comprehensive set of beliefs has mass appeal precisely because it is comprehensive. He speaks for many who seek, in him, the amplification of their own freedom of speech and who are happy in that cause to relinquish their independence of thought. The subscription to traditionalism is unqualified, and imagination – nowhere more so than in London – has atrophied.

What do the people who work and live in the City want? What does 'vernacular' mean to a growing city? These questions must be addressed if the 'community approach' championed by the Prince of Wales is to apply indiscriminately. Medieval street patterns look great on tea towels; you can screen out the traffic and dress the people like those on the Quality Street tin.

*

There is an invisible force-field over London, 100 metres above pavement level. New buildings aspiring higher than this will perish and their authors will be punished for impertinence. For 100 metres is the approximate height of St Paul's Cathedral, and the new force-field is the first tangible evidence of planning by royal consent.

As the inheritor of a – in fact, *the* – symbol of national pride and tradition, the Prince of Wales has taken a keen interest, vocational as well as personal, in the environmental sanctity of St Paul's. His public appeal for views of the building to be protected and for the area around it to be scaled down has been the decisive factor in establishing a new set of priorities.

Despite the tall buildings which have appeared on London's skyline since the war, it is the majestic dome of Sir Christopher Wren's Baroque masterpiece which still dominates. Once the symbol of an enduring faith in the City, it is now the symbol of another. Faith in the 'modern' City is defined by the Prince in terms of how visible the cathedral is from a distance. Memories of St Paul's standing defiant amid the blaze and rubble of the Blitz are invoked. The Luftwaffe is depicted as a destructive force, but one that is to be preferred to the more cold-blooded evil of modern development, which has caged our national treasure in a tomb of concrete and glass.

Half a century on from Winston Churchill's directive that St Paul's be saved at all costs, we have its echo. Preserving the views of St Paul's is the first premise in the Prince's vision of London. It is now enshrined in the City's local plan and has been endorsed by the secretary of state for the environment.

Concern for the future setting of St Paul's was reawakened by the proposals to develop Paternoster Square, the unloved 1960s office precinct which looked groovy enough on the opening credits of *The Power Game* but has since dated badly. In March 1987 a group of developers, the Paternoster Consortium, announced a short list of architects to produce a masterplan for the site. It had been acquired from the Church Commissioners.

Seven practices were in the running. Their outline proposals were to be shown to an extraordinary assessor: the Prince of Wales.

At the invitation of the developers, the competing plans were revealed to him in June. As well as exercising his own preference, the Prince had the added burden of acting as tribune, for the public was not to be shown the entries. At the same time, he had sought and found some excellent and unanimous advice which would add architectural weight to his intuitive dislike of high buildings. The logic was faultless: why make niggling comments about schemes that are already halfway there when you can intervene at the crucial, formative stage? Anyone in the Prince of Wales's position would have done the same.

The official assessors, who had been appointed to judge the relative merits of the short-listed concepts, thought Arup Associates and the Richard Rogers Partnership should be joint winners. The Arup scheme featured an 'inhabited wall' which screened off the bulk of office development; the Rogers solution had, as its centrepiece, an underground station in the middle of the square. Passengers would emerge via escalators and catch their first glimpse of the cathedral through a giant glass atrium in the form of an inverted pyramid. The developer, though, invoked 'promoter's choice' and named Arup as the sole winner – after the Prince of Wales had 'vetted' the schemes. One of the assessors, Charles Jencks, complained that royal intervention had turned the selection into a political choice. After a short period during which it looked as though the two practices would join forces to work on the masterplan, Richard Rogers resigned when it became clear that the Prince had marshalled fierce opposition to any overtly interventionist scheme for the site.

The Prince was unimpressed with the way the competition had gone and privately encouraged a 'rogue' solution by John Simpson and Partners, a rigidly classical scheme which deferred to St Paul's and which was openly historicist in its appeal. In the week when the Prince attacked all seven short-listed schemes in his speech to City planners at Mansion House – in December 1987 – John Simpson's beautifully drawn alternative surfaced. Nobody disguised the fact that this was the Prince's choice – indeed, the Prince plugged it in the speech.

The Simpson scheme was a classical purée of elements from

Inigo Jones, John Soane, Christopher Wren, Uncle Tom Palladio and all. Thanks to the Prince, an emotional and unsolicited response to the official winner of the design competition was now up and running. Pressure on the developers secured pride of place at the public exhibition, held in the crypt of St Paul's, for a model of the Simpson scheme. While Arup was bounced into showing what appeared to the public as esoteric masterplan doodlings, Prince Charles's demand for a 'public debate' saw to it that Simpson's scheme stole the show. For all the talk of public involvement in the democratic planning process, from both developer and Prince, the battle for Paternoster had become a private struggle between them. It was new versus old, and while the final appearance of Paternoster Square had yet to be resolved, the tide was beginning to turn.

While the Big Bang had encouraged the City to adopt a more *laissez-faire* development policy to allow the Square Mile to respond to the challenge of a new financial quarter in the Isle of Dogs, the Big Whimper of Black Monday had slammed the machine into reverse. All the signs were there that planners would pursue a more conservationist goal and scale down ambition.

An important test case decided in April 1989 underlined the central importance of the Prince's view of London as a museum piece. A local inquiry had been held into appeals by developers Wates City Properties against refusal for an office scheme at London Wall, the most contentious aspect of which was an office tower 108 metres high – eight metres higher than St Paul's. The City contended that the building would ruin the view of St Paul's from Waterloo Bridge, a breach of the Prince's eleventh commandment. Not that the office block would come between the viewer and the cathedral (it would be behind it), but the building would be an inappropriate backdrop and screen out the sky.

The Environment Secretary, Nicholas Ridley, shared the concern over spoiled views and passed the issue back to the City, which was told it could impose a 'comprehensive set of conditions' for the detailed design. A precedent has now been set: under the City's local plan, there will be no development in excess of the 5:1 plot ratio, historic buildings will be protected from development which is too close or too unsympathetic, and there will be no high buildings.

'The City does not need any more high landmark buildings,' said City planner Peter Rees, when the test decision was announced. 'It already has St Paul's and the NatWest Tower, God and Mammon.'

So that's it. That's our allocation of tall buildings. The London skyline is like one of those visual puzzles which contain two images (is it an old hag or a young woman?) and which are decipherable only if you discount one and concentrate on the other. If you look at a Canaletto painting of London, as the Prince of Wales has, and then look at the skyline as it is today, you will notice that the twentieth century has had the nerve to produce a number of tall buildings. But simply because St Paul's unique dominance of the skyline has been challenged does not mean that the building itself has been conquered. It is still the best building on the skyline, and it is big enough to stand up for itself.

However diverting this architectural version of 'Kim's Game' is for the anti-modernists (what buildings are missing from this nineteenth century engraving?), its ultimate aim is to change nothing. If, however, you look at the skyline as it is now – no going back! – and compare it to the way it *could* look, the tall buildings appear pretty meagre and few. In terms of composition, which is after all the criterion by which London is judged by some to be overdeveloped, the skyline would benefit from more and larger buildings. The Prince of Wales put his finger on it when he described the doomed Mies tower for Mansion House Square as 'a glass stump'. The reason so many tall buildings look inadequate is that they are indeed too 'stumpy'. Make them *bigger*.

Despite the horror which greeted the public inquiry inspector's report and the decision to approve by Ridley, the scheme to replace mediocre Victorian buildings at Mansion House Square (now No. 1 Poultry) with a new scheme by James Stirling, Michael Wilford and Associates is a minor victory for common sense in the context of the city as a whole. Conservationists claim that the Stirling design was treated as a special case: the inspector, Brian Bagot, said that, 'The designation of conservation areas is not in my opinion intended as a means to secure the preservation of buildings that are not judged worthy of statutory listing', and that the Stirling design might produce a masterpiece. Yet the unique arguments in favour of the Poultry scheme prove it to be the exception to the rule.

This successor to the grand plan for a Mies tower is on a much smaller scale, and was described – oddly – as looking like a '1930s wireless set' by the Prince. But London buildings do not have to be tall to upset the Prince. His most damning criticism of a modern building was reserved, in his *Vision of Britain*, for Sir Denys Lasdun's National Theatre. 'I've tried very hard to persuade myself to appreciate that. I can't . . . I can't,' he confessed.

In the autumn of 1988, the National Theatre was granted use of the appellation 'Royal'. The timing could not have had more dramatic irony. While the Queen was inside, bestowing the title on a national institution justly honoured for a quarter of a century of peerless artistic endeavour and triumph, her son was revealing the depth of his contempt for the building itself. He described the theatre as looking like a nuclear power station.

Six months later, the administrators of the (R)NT were castigated by a spluttering *Sunday Telegraph* for continuing to use old stocks of writing paper with 'no mention of Royal . . . shouldn't the theatre be more proud of its new name?'

The reverse may also be argued: shouldn't the Prince of Wales be more proud of the theatre? It is, of course, right that the Prince should speak out so unequivocally on a matter that clearly moves him. I, too, claim that right. I believe the National Theatre to be among the most exciting and vigorous London buildings of the century; it was a great thrill for me to have been able to present Lasdun with the RIBA award for the NT when I was chairman of the Institute's London Region in the 1970s. Lasdun has put up with some pretty wounding observations on what I believe to be his masterpiece. It is almost impossible to find anyone who feels lukewarm about the building. You either love it or hate it.

Gleefully pursued for his reaction to the Prince's disapprobation, and with the threat of a major internal redesign being actively discussed by a financially hard-pressed administration, Lasdun said:

When I began on the National Theatre building my main hope was to see if architecture could serve drama in today's terms – and to make a place which was nevertheless convivial and congenial. Over almost eighteen months we discussed this project with Olivier, Peter Hall, William Gaskill, Peter Brook, Ken Tynan ... you name them, they were all involved – the greatest intelligences the theatre had to offer. These discussions were the point of departure for the whole design. And there were many trials and errors before we came to an answer which we thought was right.

... the National Theatre has been visited by some 5 million people, most of whom have thoroughly enjoyed the experience. This, I think, is partly because of the setting – the disposition of the foyers relative to the river and the City. If you change the atmosphere into that of a second-class hotel selling knick-knacks in the name of survival, there is a great danger of destroying the spirit that people enjoy.

An artist who can claim any authenticity has to be true to himself and what he thinks. The National was certainly an authentic building of its time, as I felt it. Of course I wouldn't do it the same now, but then I don't know what I would do until I started. I'm not a high-tech man, I'm not a rationalist or a deconstructionist or any of these -ists. I am what I am, and that is what I gave in the 1960s. It will be out of fashion and come into fashion and then go out of fashion again. These things happen to everybody, including, may I say, Sir Christopher Wren.

... In the early days of the National Theatre, I walked into the foyer and I saw people sitting on the floor drinking their coffee and beer, propped up against the columns on the carpet. From that day on I've never had any worries about it being convivial ... The architecture may be very austere, relying on proportion, space, tactile qualities – my interpretation of Classicism. But I prefer people to be in way-out clothes, looking splendid whether in jeans or tiaras – it doesn't matter – all against a rather austere background, rather than the tacky one of a hotel.'

Lasdun's 'point of departure' is the hidden agenda for all architects. While the Prince and his followers may carp about the artistic decisions made about this or that building, the whole process begins with a brief from the client. This is influenced by factors a good deal more prosaic than external appearance.

The British Library, the design of which is being led by Colin St John Wilson, has also attracted a great deal of criticism, not least from the Prince. But let us not forget that this is a government contract which has been running for more than a quarter of a century and has reflected the incredibly complex and constantly changing demands imposed by the trade winds of finance and a literary collection which is itself deteriorating at one end and expanding at the other. It is first and foremost a working building, housing millions of documents and having to accommodate a series of offices and reading rooms. The brief has been endlessly revised; the library was originally planned for a site in Bloomsbury and when a new site was acquired next to St Pancras Station, there were strict rules imposed governing access and services.

Nobody except an architect can know the extent of control over design. At the British Library, as elsewhere, the shape reflects a conscious effort by government agents to move away from 'corridor' buildings with Victorian connotations towards a new generation of buildings which use the space around them to draw in daylight. The 'daylight protractor', which made mandatory approved daylight angles for building design, fundamentally determined the overall shape of office blocks; it militated, in fact, in favour of towers. The point of departure for a government-approved scheme is considerably further on than the blank sheet of paper.

In order to codify the angles of daylight necessary to buildings in London, a system of calculation was devised which was reduced to a simple perspex protractor laid on drawings of plans and sections to determine the theoretical envelope in which a building can be designed.

The Prince extends his criticism of the Library to the interior. He shows us a drawing of a reading room and tells us it looks nothing like one. I look at the drawing and I see a large room full of books, tables and chairs. It looks *exactly* like a reading room. What the Prince means is that it doesn't look like the old reading room, the one used by Karl Marx a century ago. Now, I can get as sentimental as anyone about the old reading room when I'm not sitting in it, but as a former user I found it cold and uncomfortable and the retrieval system was slow and inefficient.

The control of buildings in inner London can be traced back to legislation following the Great Fire itself; the first rules aimed at preventing the spread of fire from building to building. There are also common-law provisions to preserve 'ancient lights', which protect daylight to a building over land owned by someone else.

It was modern technology which caused a major reappraisal. Corridor development – buildings alongside streets with a frontage and a backyard – had established a norm, however inappropriate. As soon as technology, in the form of steel frames and reinforced concrete, enabled buildings to be higher, the need for revised standards became apparent. The pre-war London County Council estates put four- and five-storey blocks close together, with the result that the interiors have a gloomy atmosphere.

After the war, the new daylighting standards – in the form of the mystical protractors – produced a series of angles and radii in three dimensions. What developers needed was the skill of an architect able to navigate a new building through the invisible obstacle course of treacherous geometry which would surround it.

Richard Seifert mastered the use of the protractors, and this determined the size and shape of many of his buildings which appeared in the 1960s. Centrepoint, for example, rises as a sharp point block from a podium to avoid infringing the daylight of other buildings around St Giles's Circus. The NatWest Tower is, likewise, a creative response to the daylighting protractors. Seifert could have gone for a site-covering building of ten storeys, say, in an irregular and uneconomic shape within the invisible envelope. His solution was, instead, a slim, elegant tower which provides the same amount of accommodation and slips neatly between the geometric boundaries.

A close examination of the fine-grained, complex city forms which the Prince of Wales so admires in Siena, for example, would reveal a comprehensive contravention of all our own daylighting standards. The fact that high-density urban development can be made to work in our own age must raise many questions about the relevance of existing standards. There must be a complete technical re-examination of necessary levels of daylight for comfort and safety in our modern commercial buildings.

How Carolean London will look is important, but not as important as how it will work. The architect is able to determine both. But unless things change, the architect is forced to work in a system which is becoming more rather than less clogged with the bureaucratic silt the Prince of Wales abhors.

I offer two snapshots for the Prince's scrapbook which illustrate what architects were up against in London in 1989. The first is of the arrival at Camden Council of the planning application for the King's Cross redevelopment, masterplanned by Norman Foster. It is being unloaded from a van and carried inside in more than fifty separate boxes. The second is of a VIP reception at the Guildhall, home of the City Corporation. In the background is a line of ceremonial pikemen in full regalia.

The question is, what have they to do with a public inquiry into plans for an office and gallery extension at Guildhall Yard East? The answer is this: English Heritage had objected to the size of the new building and had asked why it was so tall. The architect explained that the main gallery was required by the client (the City Corporation) to be used for 'pikemen's drill'. The pikemen have to parade 'with pikes in the upright position', and they needed a height of 14 feet.

It is time to change our priorities if London is not to become, by the next century, simply a tourist service industry. The Prince of Wales is trying hard to stifle new and unorthodox architecture. If he succeeds, his epitaph will be the same as that on Sir Christopher Wren's tomb: *Si monumentum requiris, circumspice*. If you seek his monument, look around you.

3
Monorail
from Albert Square

If history is rewritten, it will never forgive us. We are living through a period in which it is easier to reinterpret an apparently picturesque past than to interpret a real present. But time flies, and the old power structures are melting faster than ice-fields under an ozone hole.

The last decade has seen the world shrink to the size of a football: millions of television viewers watch a World Cup match – or a disaster – simultaneously all over the globe; information is beamed from continent to continent in the time it takes to dial a number. After ten centuries of discovering how vast the earth apparently was, we have learned in ten years how tiny it really is. Infinite horizons of progress have drawn nearer with each discovery of how close we are to environmental bankruptcy. The superpowers have carved up the land with swords *and* ploughshares, the technology of Western empires has expanded like gas in a vacuum. The once-arcane lexicon of ecology is now required reading. Space is finite, time is finite, life is finite: we are living under a low ceiling. As we approach the turn of the century, a realization is dawning that we must abandon conquest and settle. The challenge is now the quality of life.

In the United Kingdom, we are on the threshold of the new Europe, united by trade and divided by language. And although competing national interests may make it anything but a common market, we all breathe the same air. The new European standards are the Ecu and the Eco. We may still regard the Soviet Union as an unsolved mystery, but we all know the Russian for 'wormwood': Chernobyl.

Britain's economic regeneration has sharply divided 'work' and 'leisure'. We now have more time to stop and stare at the appalling state of our urban areas, and the politicians have realized that custody of the electorate will depend increasingly on their custody of the environment.

The 1990s and the early 2000s will see a continuation of the major changes now taking place in the way groups with a political purpose are formed. The decline of manufacturing industries, the rise in home ownership, the social segregation of people by age and lifestyle – these and other factors have conspired to displace traditional ideas of class and replace them with new ideas of status. If you had told community activists in the 1950s that their successors would be 'power dressing' and 'power lunching' their way through a complex maze of statutory grants and private-sector buy-ins, it would have been regarded as pure fiction. Social systems have rearranged themselves, however, to produce new formulae and a new critical mass for popular power groups. Collective action is becoming less to do with people who work together and more to do with people who live together. Central government is set for a period in which the demands for better conditions will come not from people at work but from people at home. And for many of those living in our neglected towns and cities, it is no place like home.

Membership of trade unions in the UK peaked during the winter of discontent in 1978–9 at 13.3 million. By 1983 membership had fallen to 11.3 million, a drop of 15 per cent in four years. The power of trade unionism was eroded steadily in a series of legislative moves which culminated in the Trade Union Act of 1984, and was dealt a mortal wound with the final judgement of Regina *vs* Scargill. But while a rush of private-sector investment, denationalization and the expansion of the service-industries sector has masked both the finite nature of North Sea Oil revenue and the contraction of a manufacturing base, the effects of state withdrawal from the public sector are apparent. People are beginning to realize that the Conservative Government is increasingly vulnerable on environmental issues: indeed, the Government is anxious to be seen to be taking a proactive stance on Green policies.

For most people the environment – like charity – begins at home. For those living in our inner cities, it starts just outside the front door with toxin-laden air, filthy streets and neglected buildings. It is a little shortsighted, given the Government's catalytic conversion to the ecological movement, for the Environment Secretary to complain about those who, by inference, spoil it for everyone by not wanting things spoiled for themselves: the NIMBYs. Of course people don't want ghastly new roads or unsightly development in their backyards or outside their front door. Why should they not protest?

In many ways, the environment begins and ends with the neighbourhood. There is a discernibly large gap between the universal and the specific in the current wave of environmental concern. A global television community grows more and more anxious about the greenhouse effect and disappearing rainforests; it is ruining the world for everybody and is a common concern. The kulaks of the West see jungle turned to prairie and complain that it is spoiling the view; for the peasants of the Third World it might be a reckless form of land management but it is keeping them alive. We may cheer Greenpeace and worry publicly about the disposal of toxic waste, but at home we say hello to the milkman and complain when the dustmen are late.

We are spending more and more time at home, in a schizophrenic relationship with the people we see every day: there are the real-life ones, our neighbours, and the real-as-life ones, our *Neighbours*. The TV-ratings chart is dense with soap operas and situation comedies. It is our vicarious, precarious hold on an ideal world. Living in harmony in sunny small-town Australia is a subconscious ideal now for millions of people. The role models for three generations of contemporary viewers are Charlene Robinson, Madge Ramsay and Helen Daniels. The persuasive power of *Neighbours* is that it presents us not with a real world but with an *ideal* one. The disasters are always domestic, the intrigues trivial, as in real life. But unlike the experience of many who live in our cities today, the community is a stable one: it has a resilience based on the unshakable social cohesion of suburbia and the intimacy of a commune. 'Neighbours should be there for one another; that's when good neighbours become good friends', grinds the theme song. 'Next door is only a footstep away.' Next door is only a remote-control keypad away.

While escapist fantasy has come a long way from *Peyton Place* to *Dallas* and *Dynasty*, the gritty social realism of *Coronation Street* in the 1960s has given way to the depressingly evocative *EastEnders* in the 1980s. Albert Square, at its most convincing, is indistinguishable from the real thing: London's East End *is* as squalid as this in parts – in others, worse. The people here are not part of a community but a collection of individuals, a society. In the Queen Victoria there is a young woman on the dole and a successful local businessman. They live in the same place but their problems are a world apart. What they have in common is location, the neighbourhood, the environment. What they need is an architect.

The blueprint for Albert Square exists. It is in Hackney, east London, and was taken by the creators of *EastEnders* as a prototype. Attention to detail is so important that researchers are constantly in the real world, trawling for dialogue, filming life on the streets to enable the production team to reconstruct the setting as accurately as possible.

And if the future of Albert Square is to move in parallel with the real square, it is in for a siege.

The Department of Transport and the Department of the Environment are currently studying proposals for major road routes through east London to cope with the massive pressures generated by Docklands and the Channel Tunnel. For Hackney, the consequences are crucial. There are twelve options and if the wrong one is chosen there will be no more Albert Square. It will lie under a brand-new trunk road which will slice through the neighbourhood on its way from the City to the motorway. The thousands of people who live in Hackney, who for years have had to put up with roads clogged by cars just passing through and who for years have had to put up with no Tube line and inadequate local transport, will simply be in the way. Their homes must disappear to make way for more motor cars.

Just as the real blueprint for the fictional Albert Square exists, so in the TV version we have the model for a real inner-city society coping with the ravages of neglect and the widespread problem of public space which belongs to everyone but which is looked after by nobody.

It is difficult to demonstrate how architecture, in its broadest sense, can be applied to a specific neighbourhood: everyone's patch is unique, and while slides of environmental improvements somewhere else may look impressive, people need to know how architects can effect change in *their* street.

Let us, then, take Albert Square as common ground. The location is familiar to millions of us. What could an architect do for the residents of *EastEnders*?

It is early morning in Albert Square. A newspaper delivery girl leans her BMX against the outside wall of a house and walks slowly to the front door, reading the copy of *Smash Hits* she will later drop off at Number 32. She looks up briefly to push a *Daily Mail* and the local newspaper through Dot Cotton's letterbox. Cut to interior, where Dot is in her dressing gown and on her first fag of the day. She enters the hallway, stoops to pick up the newspapers. The headlines on the front page of the local rag says something about juggernauts. By the end of the episode the angry residents are, as they say, up in arms.

The pub is alive with talk about the new road: they shall not pass! An old codger remembers Cable Street. Pauline Fowler reminisces about the area as it was before the slum-clearance programmes of the early 1960s. Good old Albert Square! They must stick together and save the Square! Several of the regulars stay on for 'afters' when Frank closes the Queen Vic for the night. Michelle and David are there, trying to persuade the others to take a rational view of the problem. Duncan remembers an architect he worked with on a grant-aided project for a boys' club; he would know how they should go about this. He'll give him a call tomorrow. Meanwhile, they should convene a residents' meeting in the community centre in two days' time to plan a strategy.

There are faint hearts among them, those who just *know* there is nothing the residents of Albert Square can do to prevent the road being built. They are disillusioned before the fight has even started. They need encouragement and motivation. It turns out that Duncan's former acquaintance now works for an architectural co-operative less than three miles away. It is a small, multi-disciplinary practice formed by architects, planners, engineers, surveyors and other consultants to act as environmental advocates for community groups and tenants' organizations. Between them, they know every trick in the book. Mike the architect is very positive when Duncan rings him. He agrees to come along to the meeting at the community centre.

It is the night of the meeting. The community centre is packed and noisy. Children bawl intermittently and there is an animated murmur among the adults. Duncan rises from his seat at the front of the hall and says a few brief words. We all know why we're here; if we stand together we can make them change their minds; the residents united will never be defeated . . . He introduces Mike. He takes the floor and immediately explains that although there has been little time to prepare any kind of background information, he has obtained a copy of the consultative document on future transport strategies for east London and has read it. He explains that there are twelve options: they range from the severest intervention – the introduction of a trunk road through Walford – to the slightest – a rigorous system of traffic management and upgraded public transport.

Albert Square must get behind Option Twelve (no road) and the residents must take a wider view. The road threatens not just them but every other neighbourhood in the borough. There must be a consensus of opinion among all the community groups in the area; they must unite to oppose the road plan. Mike promises to contact other residents' associations and tenants' groups in the borough with a view to a public meeting at which they can share their ideas for opposition. Everyone agrees that Option Twelve should be implemented now, regardless of what is eventually decided. For a year, a ruthless regime of traffic management must be imposed along the stretch of existing main road and its subsidiaries, which are deemed by the transport authorities to be inadequate for the task facing them: heavy penalties and instant removal for any car left parked on the carriageway, routes designated for buses only, residents' parking permits. Public transport must be improved, greatly, with easier fare structure and more frequent buses. There is no Tube line either . . .

The borough's community groups get together and offer fierce resistance to the road proposals. Although the transport authorities are not prepared to comment on the short list of options now being prepared, they have agreed to another round of consultation. Nothing major is going to happen in the Albert Square area for three years. Mike the architect brings the news to a meeting of residents in the Queen Vic. Everyone is relieved, but strangely deflated. What do they do now: simply wait and see what long-term plans will be handed down to them? The experience of acting together as a group has focused a collective attention on the state of their neighbourhood. Is it worth saving? Or will the powers that be simply see another squalid, run-down, bashed-about and patched-up Victorian backwater? They ask Mike who is keen to keep the motivation of the group going and believes that life in Albert Square could radically improve, given a common will. He asks them what is wrong with Albert Square as it is, and they tell him – the environment. They love their homes and their neighbours but hate the setting.

The architect makes a list of grievances. Two lists, in fact. The important one contains the things that affect *everybody*. Broken paving slabs, filth and litter, the abandoned car on the corner, the black polythene sacks full of rubbish that the council won't take away, the new stallholder in the market who refuses to co-operate with the others and leaves cardboard boxes in the street, the appalling state of the small patch of public open space in the middle of the square which is unkempt and abused, the graffiti, the crime. The residents are animated because, as the complaints spill out, the architect tells them that these are all things that can conceivably be eradicated. He suggests a day trip to the neighbouring borough, where a comprehensive environmental improvement programme, initiated and overseen by the residents themselves, has transformed an area similar in scope.

Inside their homes, some of the residents have leaking roofs, others have rising damp, others can't afford to run the heating system. The flats of the old and the poor are suffering from fuel poverty and have condensation. These problems affect *some* of the residents. Dog shit on the pavement: that affects all of us. A few are unemployed and others have part-time work; the consequences of a struggling local economy affect everyone. There are a few car owners, but for the majority of residents, public transport is essential.

'Sort out Albert Square.' Would an architect take that brief from people who don't even own the land? A good architect would. It is now possible for anyone to call in an architect and say, 'I don't like where I live but I want to stay there', and for that to make sense. The architect's brief these days embraces sociology, geography, group dynamics and economics. Architecture is a social force, and it is becoming less theoretical and more practical. It is increasingly intuitive and is reaching a wider audience, thanks to the popularization of the debate since Prince Charles's intervention. We may quarrel with his subjective judgements on matters of taste and style, but he is absolutely right to call for architecture to be put under the feet of the people and not over their heads. His encouragement to self-help groups has been twofold. First, he has helped to establish – both in his public speeches and in the practical aid given to inner-city communities through the Prince of Wales Trust – that people *themselves* can change the way they live; with the right professional help, they can formulate their own plans for urban renewal. Second, his campaigning has given impetus to the growing awareness that the neighbourhood is the critical mass. A council block, a street, a square, a village: a body of people who can maintain personal contact throughout the project is a formidable force, as local authorities have discovered and national politicians are acknowledging.

Back to Albert Square. Mike the architect is capable of producing an urban analysis for the residents in a month. He may at this stage require a formal relationship with a 'client' and the residents may be asked to form a trust, to which is delegated the power of negotiation. Mike is working on spec, receiving no fee as yet, but he will log out his time against future payment if he is successful in getting grant aid or private investment for an improvement scheme. The analysis will show the ownership and tenure of land in the neighbourhood: large chunks of it will be owned by the local authority; another lump may be in the hands of the Gas Board, say. The insides of the buildings are not discussed at this stage.

The analysis is of the current condition of Albert Square and its environs and would examine how people move through the streets how they get to work and school, where the cars are parked and how much space is designated for that purpose, the number and condition of houses in the Square and the immediate neighbourhood. The architect produces a mass of information in a painstaking and often tedious process of statistical harvesting. It is worth it, though, because now the fun really starts.

At the next meeting between residents and the architect, the information has to be shared in as comprehensible a way as possible. But the task is not simply to inform; it is to inspire. It needs an outsider to see Albert Square not only as it is but as it could be. People have become so used to the depressing no man's land under the railway viaduct that it has become part of the landscape. It is the architect's job to convince his clients – his potential employers – that almost anything is possible. You cannot simply dump a folder full of drawings and diagrams on the table and ask the community what they want you to do next. The architect must encourage people to see an unimagined potential in their everyday surroundings. It is a big mistake to start an environmental campaign by drawing up modest objectives. Initially, there may be nothing but moderate suggestions from the people on how things could get better. To start with, though, better is not good enough. Best is best. Interpersonal skills are much more important to the architect than the ability to draw. It is impossible to be a good architect and be 'bad with people'.

We all take our homes for granted, to a greater or lesser extent. An architect must never do this with other people's homes. It is amazing how little most of us know about the history of our neighbourhood, what has shaped it, what is beneath our feet. To warm up the meeting, Mike may list, in the style of a tabloid newspaper, 'Ten Things You Never Knew about Albert Square'. Did you know that the land was ceded originally by a charter of Henry VI to the local monks as part of a political deal which in many respects was not unlike the modern horsetrading at London Docklands? Did you know that there are four times as many people living in Albert Square now as there were when it was built? Did you know there was a major brick-built Victorian trunk sewer that cuts through the south-west corner of the Square, so big you could drive a coach and four along it? (Explain later to Ethel that nobody's actually *tried* it.) Did you know that your rubbish is collected by Walford Borough Council and tipped on to barges which then take it all out into the Thames estuary and dump it? And so on.

After a thorough analysis of Albert Square as it is come the questions. If everybody here at the meeting owned all the land, what would you do with it? This is often a real eye-opener. Those who accuse architects of being elitist should sit in on one or two residents' meetings. Our job is to get aspirations aimed as high as possible and many of our prompts may seem bourgeois and middle class. This is understandable, as many of us are bourgeois and middle class. The more you attend meetings of community groups, however, the more you realize that the class syndrome is not merely the professional's prerogative. The brilliant urbanist Denise Scott-Brown, in her pioneering work with inner-city groups in Memphis, realized that goals are common: 'I've never met a residents' planning committee that didn't have middle-class aspirations.' People want landscaping and porches on their front doors, they want a steady income and a standard of environment that matches the adverts for posh cars. For the Albert Square scheme, porches are peripheral at this stage; core issues must be settled. Are you happy with the condition of your house or flat? Do you need a pub? And a wine bar? And another wine bar? What shops are needed locally? How important are the café and the laundromat? What about the church? Duncan is keen to involve the 'parish' in community affairs. What land and buildings does the church own and how can they be brought into fuller use?

The architect must be challenging. He is neither a servant nor a philanthropist. He is an agent and he must be provocative: You want *what*? You want a little red Hoppa bus to take you to Hackney Marshes at the weekend? But you're living in a district which has been wilfully ignored by the transport authorities for decades. There's no Underground station for miles. The buses take ages to shuffle along crowded roads. You're two minutes as the crow flies from the City of London, a world financial centre where people are making a small fortune just selling sandwiches to the people making large ones. You don't need a Hoppa bus. You need a monorail link from Albert Square to Bank. The City of London uses your neighbourhood as a tradesman's entrance while it amasses wealth beyond imagination. With a monorail you could be in the City in ten minutes, tapping in to where the jobs are . . .

There is a long vertical drop between the aims of a Hoppa bus and a monorail. One is clearly achievable, the other is a dream. But if that's what Albert Square needs – and only the people who live there can finally decide that – then that's what should be aimed for. In reality, we'll settle for an Underground station and lower bus fares and Hoppa buses to Hackney Marshes, but let's aim high and go in hard. The people of the East End (like those of Tyneside, Merseyside, Glasgow, Cardiff) have been pushed around by economics all the way from the nineteenth-century Canary Wharf to the twenty-first-century Canary Wharf.

Albert Square must proceed with its masterplan, irrespective of who owns the land or buildings. The brewery owns the Queen Victoria, but that doesn't stop the residents deciding that they need the pub enlarged and made less of an adults' drinking-hole and more of a community, family facility. There should be an extension at the back to accommodate a family room. There needs to be a lock-up shed for the market traders to store their gear – that can go on the corner site of a former London Electricity Board substation which is now surplus to LEB requirements . . . After the monorail idea, there has been one major question hanging in the air like smoke in the snug: where is the money coming from? Initially, a whip-round for Mike among the residents would help. His main fee will be paid when a developer is found.

Final funding arrangements are not important at this stage. It is much more important to generate ideas and construct a vision of Albert Square which meets the demands of the people who live there. If the ideas are good enough, the money will come. And the ideas, though strong, must also be vague enough not to trap everybody into considering a scheme which is set in stone before it has even started. Nowadays architects use drawings increasingly as metaphors and are unlearning the habit of drawing too much too soon. In formulating concepts, drawings are useful primarily as generators of ideas, not as realizations. Architects are now learning to think rather than draw, because however catholic an architect's imagination, once drawn never forgotten. It is often very difficult to prevent the sketch becoming the solution.

Although we feel comfortable about the notion of designing 'with a community', the complex relationships which evolve between the architect and the residents soon make it clear that what we are dealing with is a society, with its own hidden hierarchical structures and political nuances. The architectural response must reflect a diversity of needs and demands. It is pointless at an early stage to present finely drawn pictures of a new community centre. The residents must be stimulated by halftones and guidelines which encourage them to have their *own* vision of what they want to see. After two or three consultations, the architect will bring together a masterplan.

It shows the whole of Albert Square and the surrounding neighbourhood. It shows a park in the centre, replanted and landscaped and overseen by the vigilant neighbours; a road closure here; garages there; part of the church converted to a multi-purpose hall. It shows some of the larger houses divided into two to provide sheltered housing, with a warden's flat so that older members of the society (like Ethel and Willy) can remain and not be shunted off to an old folks' home in another part of the borough. It shows a block of local-authority flats which have gone for changed tenure under the 1988 Housing Act and are now managed by a tenants' co-operative housing association, which has received a municipal dowry to carry out its own rehabilitation scheme. It shows a new building on the redundant plot of land owned by the Gas Board; a block of workshops and offices constructed under the B1 Use Classes Order to create local employment. Ozcabs now operates from one of the workspaces; Rod has set up a band-management and equipment-hire firm with a seedcorn grant from the Prince's Youth Business Trust; Ian runs his catering business from an office there. James Wilmot-Brown's ill-conceived wine-bar conversion has gone and in its place is a modern 'footprint' office complex, 3,000 square feet of high-tech development with Dr Samuels's new surgery on the ground floor and a centre for the health visitors and itinerant midwives attached. Patel and Lo, a local firm of solicitors, are interested in taking one of the spaces. Half the Square is closed to traffic, with a discreet new three-storey car park built behind nearby flats.

By the time this kind of masterplan is put before the EastEnders, around three months has elapsed since the first meeting. At this point, consensus is needed on a detailed strategy. Assuming that the masterplan is agreed, the architect will start trawling for developers and start consulting the local-authority planners. He has deliberately left council planners out of the first-stage conceptualization, because their development-control policy would simply get in the way and introduce a negative effect on the ambitions of residents. The architect has, however, read all the local plans, the structure plans, the whole anthology of environmental codes that affect the area, and is able to present the planner with a sound, commercially based scheme for regeneration which does not contravene the rules. If the planner objects, the reservations will be expressed not to an isolated and elitist consultant but to the residents themselves. What is important is to keep the negative influences at bay for as long as possible.

The architect must act as a marriage broker, bringing together those who own land which they don't need and those who are prepared to invest for a financial return – the landowner and the developer. The architect must also help residents to orchestrate public opinion with a sound marketing strategy. Do we go public with the new-look Albert Square before we talk to the local authority, before we talk to the landowners? The architect must weigh the advantages and disadvantages of risking injured municipal pride and the proprietorial umbrage of statutory property boards against the psychological edge of a community as prime mover. It is a matter of delicate judgement. Developers will respond to a community that knows what it wants, the statutory undertakers will dispose of land (sometimes for a taste of the action) if it is commercially viable. But the impetus must come from a genuine public will to see things happen. As we move into the 1990s, this convergence of interest will become a steadily more persuasive formula for urban regeneration because its credentials, fundamentally, are impeccable: it is what the people who live there want. The architect's role is to set ambition at as high a level as possible.

Could it ever happen? There is a far greater chance of a local urban renewal programme, devised by residents and an architect for a small area of inner city, happening now than ever before. There is a private sector looking for fresh opportunities, a municipal power structure fragmenting into smaller and smaller areas of responsibility, and a growing public awareness that popular action works. Architects are not alchemists, but they do understand environmental science; they know that in order to provoke a larger reaction, a catalyst must be introduced to start the process.

While the pursuit of funding goes on, the community must not wait. Things that can be done to improve the environment must be done now. For relatively little outlay, a road can be narrowed with a couple of chicanes and trees can be planted in the pavement. Flagstones can be repaired, grass can be cut and long-term litter removed. The brewery can be pressurized into a family conversion and the police pressurized into leaving their Pandas down at the nick and *walking* round Albert Square so they can see and hear at first hand what crimes are being committed in their absence. If there is no money to carry out the first, cosmetic improvements, it must be raised. If the society living in Albert Square wants commitment from the private sector and the public authorities, it too must demonstrate its commitment to the neighbourhood. By the time Angie Watts returns, ready to turn over yet another new leaf as the merry widow, she will find that Albert Square has established its own community-bond scheme – treasurer Arthur Fowler – to help fund the first-stage landscaping. Carmel is already planning a series of fund-raising events, including a Caribbean carnival and a local aerobics marathon in what used to be the old community hall and is now the new sports and fitness centre.

'Well,' says Angie, 'the old place doesn't change, does it?'

'Oh, it will,' says Mo (just back from the cash and carry and ready to start her new career as manager of the vegetarian restaurant). 'We've got big plans for Albert Square.'

She shows her a copy of the works programme; the new work-shops and offices go on site next month.

'You're joking! My God, whatever next?'

'A monorail.'

4

Holism and Homoeopathy

The start of the Carolean age will mark the start, for architects, of the 'space age'. It will signal the end of the public perception of architects as people who design buildings and the beginning of an era in which architects are seen to design space itself. It is a crucial idea, and one which modernism failed to communicate.

Architects have for too long been shackled to a public image which portrays them as designers of buildings; this is incompatible with the pressing demands for rehabilitation of the social sector. The lessons learned from the failure of high-rise high-density housing and the success of low-rise high-density housing are all to do with the *spaces* around the buildings themselves and, in a more relevant sense, the degree of control allowed to architects in determining both. And, most importantly, in determining both together.

The velocity of development in the late 1980s in Britain was almost entirely fuelled by private-sector investment. Enterprise found a common denominator throughout society, from the Sainsbury Wing of the National Gallery to the tribe of London football fans who waved wads of notes at Newcastle supporters and chanted 'Loads a money!' By the year 2000, the amount of risk capital may have settled long ago to a lower investment table.

If, as many observers predict, the issue of environment – both urban and global – is to dominate politics from now until the end of the century, the issue of how we live in our cities and how much we spend on the public realm will be of consuming interest to an electorate increasingly anxious about microwave Earth.

As the market demands of the 1980s were all about wealth, so the demands of the Carolean age will be about quality of life. It is currently acceptable for people to pay annual rent of £65 a square foot for office buildings surrounded by rubbish and dirt and traffic.

The urban setting of expensive buildings is being made to look shabbier and shabbier; putting up yet more expensive buildings merely widens the gap between penthouse and pavement. Architects as a profession face a corporate challenge not simply to produce individual buildings of higher quality but to improve the quality of the urban environment as a whole. This requires three elements:

1. Many billions of pounds.
2. A comprehensive architectural vision.
3. Many billions of pounds more.

If we are to rescue the public realm and return it to the public, we have to start thinking big. Just as the scale of inner-city problems is talked up, the scale of the solution must take a wider scope. Seen over a period of time, and from a distance, the city has certain metabolic characteristics and is vulnerable to a complex series of malfunctions. Overcrowding, poverty, bad planning, pollution, crime, fear and loneliness are the urban malignancies.

The Prince of Wales has quite properly focused our minds on the appalling conditions in which some of our people live. He suggests that the answer to urban regeneration may lie in the outward ripples from community architecture schemes or patches of office development designed with classical façades. But we must beware of confusing two fashionable forms of treatment in our diagnosis of urban decline. The Prince of Wales is familiar with both. The first is homoeopathy, which won't work. The second is holism, which will.

Homoeopathy is a system of treating diseases by administering minute quantities of medical compounds which excite symptoms similar to those of the disease. The body, taking its cue from the biochemical signal, is tripped into a cure. The parallel is an urban solution which seeks to inspire regeneration by offering isolated model developments. The invigorating vitality of the refurbished street or the Inigo Jones boutique throws the surrounding squalor into starker contrast, makes it even less acceptable. The city pulls itself together and brings everything else up to the same standard. It could work, but it would take a century.

Holism, however, is a system which examines and treats the

condition of the whole organism on the understanding that a bio-
logical malfunction is an expression of a general disorder. It stands
on the theory that the fundamental principle of the universe is the
creation of complete and self-contained systems, from the atom to
the planet. If the city is sick, we must treat the city and not Acacia
Avenue. If the national urban fabric is sick, we must treat the
nation.

We need two million new homes in Britain by the end of the
century. Fact. We had better get on with it.

The city's vital organs are the civic and government buildings,
large offices where many of our residents and commuters spend
such a huge proportion of their lives, and the institutional and
industrial buildings – the latter once again finding their way back
to the inner cities through the relaxation of town-planning controls.
And at the heart, beating a little feebly of late, the enduring presence and symbolism of the Church. It was the social generator of
all our historic towns and cities, differentiated in childhood by the
presence or absence of a cathedral.

The city's veins and arteries are now clogged and silted with
traffic, which moves slowly through, poisoning as it goes. The
plasma, though, is the population itself. There is a daily infusion
of commuters and a daily excursion at going-home time. The
people who remain, who live and work in the city, have the same
right to hearth and home as their suburbanite colleagues. But while
those who live in the satellite towns and the countryside have a
home to go to, too many of our city dwellers have only housing to
go to. And too many have no home to go to at all.

Many architects who enter the profession do so because they
are drawn to the eternal problems of housing: at its very best it
combines artistic expression, social responsibility and a practical
contribution to an improving world.

In 1988 40 per cent of all the work done by architects was in
the field of housing. Since the economic recession in the early
1970s, which effectively marked the end of political housing initiative, architects have been among the prime movers in promoting
social concern about inner-city housing. We now live in the length-
ening shadow of housing legislation which has far-reaching impli-

cations for all social housing in this country. A sweeping act of parliament has paved the way for the most dramatic change in housing provision since the great public housing acts which followed the Second World War. The mass demunicipalization of our housing stock and the promotion of private rented accommodation as a commercial market force are among the most comprehensive social changes the city will have to endure during the last decade of the millennium.

In their Christmas 1988 report on homelessness Shelter drew attention to the magnitude of the urban housing problem. Something like 370,000 people were accepted as homeless by local authorities in 1987, but that official figure is widely regarded as a gross underestimate. The overall number of homeless people in Britain is likely to be as high as 1 million.

The number of homeless households virtually doubled between 1979 and 1987. After 1982, local authorities no longer had enough permanent lettings to cope with the rising numbers of homeless people and the use of temporary accommodation – particularly the bleak bed and breakfast hotels – increased rapidly. Indeed, enterprise Britain articulated itself in the bed and breakfast sector to an impressive degree.

Landlords found a way to cut through the red tape that binds this country from end to end with an alacrity even Prince Charles might envy, were it not for the motivation. One enterprising bed and breakfast entrepreneur drove down from his Morecambe Bay establishment last Christmas and filled a van with homeless people he found sleeping rough at London's Embankment. He sorted out the necessary paperwork for social security payments, then filled his hotel, which, like the rest of Morecambe in winter, is not exactly bustling. Local people who signed a petition of objection were angry, not at the exploitation of the plight of the homeless but at the undesirable elements which had lowered the tone of the area. They needn't have worried. Homeless people are welcome at such establishments only in the absence of spending guests. The advent of warm weather usually restores the neighbourhood to a genteel normality.

Local-authority spending on temporary accommodation for the

homeless rose from £45 million in 1985–6 to £101 million the following year: more than double. In 1987–8 London authorities alone spent £100 million. A report from the Audit Commission on local councils and homelessness concluded: 'As many as three quarters of local authorities currently using bed and breakfast accommodation could end their use altogether and provide a better standard of temporary accommodation at lower cost.' This can be done now with the help of architects, who are standing by and ready to go.

The figures are shocking enough but it is the accumulated tragedy, the personal suffering of the homeless, which diminishes the whole city. The groups of people who are most severely affected by homelessness are the single, the young, women with children, ethnic minorities and homosexual men and women. One million people without a home. A holistic approach to the problem of urban living would start, as the community architects demand, from the bottom up. But the bottom is not those who live in houses which could be improved with a grant; it is those without a home at all.

We need 2 million homes by the end of the century; and what is happening? In 1978 the total number of houses constructed in England and Wales by local authorities was 71,317, a hopelessly inadequate figure. But in stark comparison, nine years later, in 1987, the figure was only 23 per cent of that: 16,412.

The School of Advanced Urban Studies, in research commissioned by the Association of District Councils in 1988, found that an additional 50,000 homes were needed to rent or buy at low cost just to cope with homelessness and the backlog of council waiting lists.

In the same year the Association of Metropolitan Authorities estimated that £86.5 billion – all the revenue expected from domestic and overseas tourism in Britain for the next six years – was needed to repair and improve all the country's housing.

In the closing years of the twentieth century, the architectural profession is again finding its voice and the self-confidence to instruct. The image of the architect has suffered from the shortcomings of municipal landlords and housing managers in the

1960s. But the 1960s are more than a generation away now, the housing produced by both public- and private-sector architects in the last fifteen years has been of the highest order, as the housing design awards show. However tentative the stylistic developments have been and whatever the current debate over tenure, architects have been among the first in society to recognize the importance of working closely with the community to achieve housing which satisfies their needs. Sheltered housing for all is an essential political goal and must be the prime objective for a civilized society.

However, the definition of adequate housing is not static. The post-war momentum to seek steadily increasing standards has been lost and must be re-established. Homes should not be seen simply in terms of numbers. The standard of housing built today should attempt to address future needs and uses rather than just respond to immediate pressures. The design challenge for the next ten years is to ensure that the 2 million new homes needed by the year 2000 offer something more than the nondescript boxes of the kind too often produced by the private house-building industry, a sector on which so much of the future, under the 1988 Housing Act, apparently depends. The democratic process has given the Government complete control over housing policy. It continues to back away from the real problem of providing low-cost housing for those in our society who are in the greatest need.

There are signs of a growing recognition in Whitehall that as the debate centres more firmly on the quality of our environment, either some fundamental ideas or those who hold them must disappear. We must be fearful of the consequences of the 1988 Housing Act. We must not accept the status quo.

It is not, I suggest, mere coincidence that the organized Church has been among the most vocal of the Government's critics and one of the most strident campaigners for housing reform and urban renewal. The publication of the *Faith in the City* report did much to restore the city's faith in the Church. The Church Urban Fund is building on the long experience of the Church as an integral part of our inner city and its timeless witness on behalf of the poor. Indeed, in many places the Church is the only major institution not to have withdrawn from the more derelict urban areas. It has been supported with great loyalty by its members there. Giving in urban churches is, on average, at a very much more generous level than that in more comfortable neighbourhoods. A new generation of highly active priests and spiritual leaders has made its presence felt in community campaigns all over the country.

There are those who predict a spiritual renaissance in response to the coming millennium. A new king will also bring us a new head of the Church of England; the environmental debate is heading for a widening of the debate about the qualities of life itself, including its spiritual quality. The Prince fears the modern world has been marked by 'the denial of God's place in the scheme of things'. I agree. I differ, though, in the interpretation of this lack of faith. The Prince of Wales says modern architecture rejects the notion of a human soul and its contribution of a force which is 'irrational, unfathomable and mysterious'. He says the way forward is to enhance the natural environment. But surely it is in the built environment that we may celebrate all the gifts and vision of human experience to glorify God.

The difference between a thriving city population and huddled masses is architecture. Not the architecture of self-seeking and isolated private schemes, but an urbanistic approach which treats the city as a whole. A key to the survival of the city as a plausible environment lies in the density of housing.

We have seen the Prince of Wales in east London, praising some badly designed houses with large gardens and expressing the hope that more will follow. If that happens, it will be a disaster. For the houses and gardens are at the centre of a major city, where space is precious. If a city is to function properly, people must live at its heart; the people on whom the city relies for its maintenance, smooth running and wellbeing. The density must be high. And high density, as we have seen with the more imaginative modern schemes, does not have to mean high rise or poor quality; nor does it necessarily mean no garden.

Without realistic density guidelines for our cities, the number of people housed to the acre is left to private developers, who have no overriding philanthropic interest in the wellbeing of the city as a whole but care merely for the short-term turnover on a one-off scheme.

All cities are about high densities; that is what gives them their dynamism and excitement. A certain number of inhabitants per acre overall is necessary simply to provide adequate numbers of people to service and maintain them. Shops, restaurants, theatres, pubs, cinemas: city life is unthinkable without them. They are all unsustainable with a population living at low densities.

The Greater London Development Plan set a maximum level of 100 habitable rooms per acre in the 1970s; that is utterly misguided. Architect Geoffrey Darke and his partner John Darbourne housed people at densities in excess of 200 an acre, in schemes which are still popular with tenants and owners today. This is what Darke said in 1989:

We need a planned London and some densities defined. Birmingham is regenerating successfully because its back-up population can support new facilities. If we don't maintain densities we will lose the qualities of the city that we love. Countries on the Continent are continually searching for high density to maintain the character and quality of urban life. Look at the densities they're building to now in Docklands – it's suburbia.

And suburbia belongs in suburbia. Behavioural patterns are different in cities, which presuppose a certain level of social activity in the streets, a conviviality. There is a rather sinister unspoken political agenda which argues for disinvestment in the city, a withdrawal from the public areas. Paranoia about urban violence and concern over deteriorating conditions are nourished by an official attitude of opting out. There could be an acceptance of a new form of urban life which is centred on the interior space of an individual home; social exchange is no longer necessary (or indeed possible – the shopping centre is locked up for the night) and everybody sits at home swallowing fast food and satellite TV.

Meanwhile, paranoia and violence spiral upwards in a ghastly self-perpetuating swirl. Put families, lots of them, back on the streets and the public areas can be reclaimed from the teenage gangsters and desperadoes. Politicians take a proprietorial attitude about this. I have had it suggested to me on a number of occasions that this subject is *ultra vires* for architects. But it is an architect's job to consider the implications of urban development as well as its form. Despite the worrying trend towards low-density schemes in London and elsewhere, the overall density of the capital is probably still between 150 and 200 people to the acre. We must reverse the trend and start housing at high densities again to preserve urban life.

It pays to build high-density schemes, but it also costs. The expense of housing 200 people an acre was one of the main reasons why government and local authorities introduced cost yardsticks and cut their housing budgets. The private sector today has done the same sums and decided on low density wherever possible; every developer's concern about the city ends with the site boundary.

A new development plan is needed for all our cities now to determine not the maximum housing density but the minimum to keep an urban momentum. There is a world of difference between high density and overcrowding. One attempts to create a community by giving many people adequate private space; the other simply crams too many people into too few places.

We need to increase the density of people in our cities; but we also need to reduce the density of traffic.

In the City of London it takes about four seconds to plant a message on a screen in Kyoto. And it takes, on a bad day, more than half an hour to get from the Bank of England to Centrepoint. Those of us who live in cities have watched the inexorable advance of the motor car over the last two decades. At 8.30 a.m. on a Sunday our historic city centres and medieval street patterns look attractive; twenty-four hours later they are car-clogged canyons full of carbon monoxide.

We were warned. More than a quarter of a century ago, in 1963, the Buchanan Report (*Traffic in Towns*) was published. It was formally addressed to the Minister of Transport, Ernest Marples, by Colin Buchanan and his working group of nine, four of whom – Buchanan included – were members of the Royal Institute of British Architects.

The message of the report was clear: there are absolute limits to the amount of traffic our cities can cope with. In the same year the Standing Conference on London Regional Planning echoed the warning and urged land-use planning to reduce transport demand. In short, both groups said that London would eventually grind to a standstill.

It did, on 24 November 1988. A National Union of Students' demonstration against the introduction of student loans resulted in a barricade across Westminster Bridge. Traffic for miles around was brought to a halt; there was administrative chaos.

Local and national government has failed to get to grips with this problem for over thirty years. In the 1950s and 1960s parking meters appeared for the first time on our streets. The revenue generated, we were promised, would pay for the construction of underground car parks. The money went, but the meters stayed. The policy of controlling parking with car parks and meters has failed. The London motorway box was abandoned in the 1960s. The urban motorway programme was abandoned in the 1970s.

The problems are architectural as well as political. Buildings generate travel and the relationship between the two is critical. The location of buildings, the space between and around them, vehicular segregation and car parking are all architectural considerations.

We could move traffic along faster if existing laws were properly enforced. On their own admission, the police have all but given up through lack of personnel. On-the-spot fines work well in other countries and they could work here, as some enterprising con men discovered on a lucrative trawl among gullible motorway speeders during the 1988 Christmas period.

We must also improve public transport, especially below ground, and sink a major investment in fare subsidies. Between 1982 and 1986 the number of people using the London Underground rose by 70 per cent. More than £900 million was allocated to be spent on the Tube in 1989, mainly on re-equipping, a transport euphemism for overdue maintenance. More than 800 million people travel on the Underground every year and three quarters of all central London commuters travel in by rail.

People would be willing to leave their cars at home if public transport became cheaper and more efficient. Environmental concern is growing rapidly; unleaded petrol is now widely available.

If we are to discourage the use of cars in cities, we must focus our attention on a major campaign to make public transport the more attractive and morally superior alternative. The Prince of Wales may need a red helicopter to keep up with his busy schedule, but the solution for the rest of us is the red bus pass. I and thousands of others travel every working day by bus; progress through the streets depends on how much private traffic there is. An illegally parked van can double or treble the average journey time.

The Government collects more than £15 billion a year in road and fuel taxes and excise. In 1989, the amount due to be spent on our roads was increased to a 'record' £3 billion. Since 1979 we have built only 850 miles of new road. Recent government promises of new road-building programmes are better late than never.

There would be fewer cars in our cities if we introduced a special inner-city road tax: an electronic tacograph in a private car could record every crossing of the city boundary. If people choose to do this, they should pay. The city is a place of movement. A strategic plan is long overdue for London and the South-East. Architects are uniquely capable of seeing problems as a whole and they must be involved in designing not just the buildings in which we work but the routes between them. Bringing together different land uses to allow people to 'live over the shop' is a start, but the ambition should be to bring the people themselves together with a new will to rescue our cities from the space-hogging car.

The city must get back on its feet. We must design journeys as well as destinations. There may have been jams yesterday and jams today, but there must be no jams tomorrow.

5

The Great Build-up

Peace, wrote George Bernard Shaw, is not only better than war but infinitely more arduous. The task that stretched ahead for the Attlee Government, so decisively voted in to pick up the pieces of a shell-shocked Britain, was indeed formidable.

Wisely avoiding the numbers trap, which was to commit the Labour Government of the 1960s to a grim and hasty programme of building, the Labour Government of the 1940s, despite some maverick claims by Bevanites that up to 5 million houses could be built in a decade, simply promised to build as many as possible.

Bombing had destroyed or made uninhabitable nearly half a million homes. There had been millions of slums owned by long-range landlords during the creeping Depression of the 1930s, and these had been swelled by houses which had fallen below acceptable levels of habitation during the war, when maintenance and slum clearance had been suspended. The mandate for post-war government in Britain was clear: an end to the idea of a divided nation, which exercised the mind of His Majesty's Government as much in the 1940s as it will in the 2020s. While Prince Charles's anxieties now, however, are over a nation divided by credit rating, the post-war Government had to fulfil an ambitious series of egalitarian manifesto aims. Class divided the nation and it would be eradicated; the 1949 Housing Act deleted references to the 'working classes' and created municipal landlords virtually overnight. The great ebb and flow of the housing market in post-war Britain, moving endlessly from private sector to public sector and back again, had begun. And for the private sector, the tide was out.

A Conservative minister, Duncan Sandys, had told a meeting of the RIBA Council a week before the end of the war, 'We desire as much as anyone to maintain diversity of design and scope for the individual talents of the architect. But first things must come first. The houses must go up and nothing must stand in their way.'

The Attlee Government had, by 1948, increased the production of new homes to 200,000 a year. By then, 40 per cent of the country's architects worked for government departments; most of the commissions for the rest originated from government sources. And the size of the construction workforce had doubled in the twenty years to 1951. In 1931, there had been a total of 692,000 builders, bricklayers, stone and other workers, contractors and managers. Of those, 99,000 were unemployed: 14.3 per cent. By 1951, the total number in the industry had virtually doubled to 1,203,000, and the number of unemployed had fallen to 35,000 – just 2.9 per cent of the total.

The establishment of a large-scale building programme resulted in an architecture far less glamorous than had at first been envisaged by the starry-eyed Corbusian evangelists. The post-war Hertfordshire schools rebuilding programme and the New Towns showed how prefabrication and building in bulk could be made to work in practical terms; but it was worthy and dull. The war had interrupted architectural development by putting most architects in uniform. And if the experience had sharpened their resolve to build a better world, it had also given them some hard lessons in pragmatism. You pinned up Veronica Lake on the wall above your bunk, but you loved and yearned for your wife. You might dream of building the most architecturally acclaimed private house in Europe, but the basic urge was to build. A school, a hospital, decent homes: these were, after all, what you had fought a war for. Public duty is also what you were architecturally trained for.

Fighting a peace-time war against poverty and appalling housing conditions, the Government had recruited modern methods and drafted in an army of drab buildings to keep up spirits on the home front. As the 1950s dawned, however, people were anxious to ditch the lingering war mentality of national service and demob architecture. There would be a party, a celebration, a Festival of Britain which would be both a thanksgiving for deliverance and the inauguration of a new age. Architects would be invited and told to wear their best frocks. But, as it transpired, architecture was all dressed up with nowhere to go. We were stood up.

The Festival began with the Labour Government in power and closed with the Conservatives embarking on their thirteen-year rule. The 1950s saw a flowering of those municipal estates which borrowed heavily from Continental models. An enthusiastic London County Council transferred responsibility for housing design from, incredibly, the valuer's department, where it certainly did not belong, to the architects' department, where it most certainly did. By the mid-1950s there were 300 architects at the LCC, working in autonomous cells and enthusiastically applying the new European style to a stubborn capital. Estates at Wimbledon and Roehampton – the kind of places Tony Hancock would joke about – brought a little bit of Gothenburg and Marseilles to south London. There was a reflection of the self-consciously modern approach in which architects forsook a previous generation's triple dictum of 'commodity, firmness and delight' for the new brief which demanded liberty, egality and fraternity. The young architectural lions no longer discussed fine art over a glass of Madeira at the Athenaeum but modern jazz over an espresso at the local coffee bar. Here were Absolute Beginners, smoking Gauloises and quoting Le Corbusier and Mies van der Rohe.

The Conservative Government, however, was pitching for the owner-occupier. After the failure of the 1957 Rent Act, which, instead of encouraging the revival of the private landlord, merely persuaded the existing ones to sell up, the Tories brought in the 1959 Housing and House Purchase Act to underwrite mortgages on older properties. The building society movement expanded like the Incredible Hulk. By the end of the Government's term in 1964 the realities of a private sector unable to cope with the sheer volume of new housing needed and a population increasingly informed by television that its living standard must rise had persuaded Whitehall to set up the Housing Corporation to boost the housing drive. This equivocal attitude was exploited by the Labour Party, whose straight-ahead approach in creating as many Labour-voting council tenants as possible helped win them victory. The standard of living escalator couldn't move fast enough. The new generation of homesteaders in the expanding suburbs were now hooked on imported American TV series. The two most popular genres were separated historically by a century but had the same message: dramas of the pioneering Wild Westerners and modern sitcoms set in the open-plan affluence of sophisticated US suburbanites conspired to incite a new frontier spirit.

There was a real feeling that we were on the edge of a new era. The drug of peace-time prosperity argued deeper in the minds of the first TV generation, increasingly homebound and with a growing disposable income. People who hadn't seen a banana until they were well into their teens were suddenly being flattered as consumers by a proactive marketing industry. Items were now 'de luxe' and 'luxury'; everyone wanted a patio like Dick van Dyke and vertical crazy paving round the fireplace. The next best thing was a new council flat. All hail the National Plan.

The desirable council flat was absolutely in tune with architectural preference and political ideals: high rise and modern. The new, the new. Clean, uncluttered lines and a symbolic break with the two-storey back-to-backs and Mum and Dad's 1930s sideboard. This was *modern*, like Formica kitchens, like Eddie Cochran in 'Twenty Flight Rock'. Running up twenty flights of stairs was what people bought. It was funny, being too tired to 'rock' when he got to the top. The reality was, as Eddie might have put it, 'Somethin' Else'.

Walking up tower-block stairways was a novelty that soon wore off; lifts that didn't work turned coming home into an arduous expedition. But when the lifts did work, when the buildings were cared for, modern living was IT. The tenants who moved into the fourteenth floor of the Brunswick Close Estate, Finsbury, in the early 1950s put up a plaque to its architect, Joseph Emberton. Some of the original tenants were still there when I refurbished the estate in the late 1970s, and they recalled the genuine feeling of excitement when they moved in. They were citizens of a new world.

The new Labour Government proposed the jacking up of housing starts to 500,000 by 1970. Of those, a fifth were to be realized by industrialized building methods and were to be executed by new consortia of local authorities, whose volume orders would encourage the establishment of UK factories for the largely Continental systems. The National Building Agency was set up to evaluate the systems.

The ambitious programme of renewal to which the Wilson Government had pinned its manifesto began to crack almost immediately. By mid-1966, the Treasury was urging the abandonment of the half-million annual target for new homes and was proposing that the rate of demolition be slowed down to compensate. The National Plan was revised to acknowledge a shortfall – instead of a predicted 3.5 per cent growth, only 2 per cent was being achieved. Housing Minister Richard Crossman and Chancellor James Callaghan battled in the Cabinet over the balance between private- and public-sector housing provision.

There was little time to consider the style or standard of that housing; the primary consideration was the target number. As Crossman said in his *Diaries*:

I wouldn't dream of ever cutting back public housing, and I was having the row which every effective Housing Minister has with his Chancellor. It has been going on since 1945. Nye Bevan fought it, Macmillan fought it, and now I'm fighting it. Chancellors are bound to consider housing inflationary and try to throttle us. Housing Ministers are bound to be regarded as hoggers getting more than their share. But unless we hog we are defeated by the alliance of the Chancellor and the other social service Ministers. The fact that I have now got a reputation in Cabinet as a bully and a thug is really to my credit.

The battle between quantity and quality was brief. There is a telling section in Crossman's *The Diaries of a Cabinet Minister* about a ministry visit to Basingstoke, the Hampshire town being developed jointly by an alliance of local authorities. Crossman had visited the area before and 'found the first housing there very dreary – lines of cantonments. Then I had a first warning last January that the architect of the Basingstoke Group had a wonderful new idea called Popley Two – an ambitious scheme for five-storey blocks of maisonettes. It is an extremely ingenious architectural device which provides decks for the top maisonettes ...'

There would be no private gardens but a high standard of public open space.

Housing was by now determined economically by cost yardsticks and spatially by Parker Morris standards,* a series of quality guidelines intended to set a minimum overall standard but which quickly became a maximum. At Basingstoke, the development group was applying for loan sanction to build 8,000 homes to the Popley Two design. 'I had begun to realise,' wrote Crossman, 'that largely as a result of accepting the Parker Morris standards, council housing is already becoming dangerously expensive.' Dangerously what? Crossman met the Basingstoke delegation, who reported that tenders had already gone out, and turned them down flat: 'I said I knew I was doing this terribly late in the day but I had to make an example of one scheme and I had selected Basingstoke because the architecture was good. If we allowed this one, all the other much worse architects would say they had the right to go beyond Parker Morris standards and to exceed the Ministry yardstick.'

A year later, in this climate of low-cost maximum yield which spurred on the ministry to create more and more 'battery housing' estates, a new development was started in the ravaged and slum-infested area of Canning Town. In the Nagasaki wasteland left by the bulldozers would rise the tallest blocks of flats for miles around, each named in honour of old Labour housing colleagues by the local authority bigwigs. The nine 200–foot blocks were christened on the drawing board: Abrahams Point, Ault Point, Bauckham Point, Dodson Point, Gannon Point, Hume Point, John Sopp Point, Merrit Point and Ronan Point.

* Minimum space standards for local authority housing, established in response to 'New Patterns of Living' outlined in the Government's Central Housing Advisory Committee report, 'Home for today and tomorrow'. The committee was chaired by Sir Parker Morris. The standards, first published in 1961, have now fallen into disuse.

6

After the Fall

Eyewitness: 'I was just passing the block when suddenly I saw a flash and a cloud of black smoke coming from about the twentieth floor. The top floors of the building collapsed, then the floors below fell. The flats went one after the other. A great cloud of dust went up into the air and I saw pieces of furniture tumbling from the flats; you could see yellow doors hanging open in the air.'

Eyewitness: 'The whole place shook. Suddenly our bedroom wall fell away with a terrible ripping sound. We found ourselves staring out over London. Our heads were only a matter of two feet from the eighty-foot drop. The room filled with dust, and showers of debris and furniture were plunging past us. Suddenly we heard screams. I think it must have been someone falling with the debris.'

It was early morning on Thursday, 16 May 1968, in east London. Night watchman George McArthur was coming to the end of his shift. He was making tea in a little hut just yards from a twenty-two-storey block of flats called Ronan Point.

There was an explosion. I heard cracking and banging and I saw concrete flying around. I ran like hell. I thought it was an explosion at the docks and then I looked up and I could see smoke coming from the top of the building. A whole wing of the building came down like a pack of cards.

The phrase was devastating in its power and simplicity. For newspaper sub-editors and politicians it proved irresistible. Within a matter of days those words and the terrifying picture over which they blazed had burned into the nation's conscience.

The story was packed with human drama – the Englishness of it, with everyone making tea. While Mr McArthur was brewing up, east London was bleary-eyed, shuffling to the door to fetch the pinta milka day they'd ordered, preparing to go to work on an egg and a cuppa. Eighteen floors above the night watchman's hut, in Number 90, Miss Ivy Hodge was putting the kettle on. 'I don't remember turning on the gas, nor lighting a match. The next moment I was on the floor. There were flames everywhere and I remember staggering to the door of my flat. Some people helped me to get out of the building.' The side of Miss Hodge's flat had blown away. The progressive collapse of the flats above produced a massive force which brought rooms in the flats below the eighteenth floor down like ... well, like a pack of cards. Four people died.

Everybody shuddered at the thought and everybody shuddered at the pictures. They showed the same stark image: a nasty, cynical, cheap and charmless tower block rent from top to bottom. Suddenly you didn't have to know how buildings were put together; you could see. This was not a machine for living in; this was a machine for being housed in. Years of corner-cutting by the housing authorities had produced buildings like this, and now a tangible corner of one of them had been ripped away. This was system building, and the harsh economic logic which devised it was clear to see. Floor slabs hung like leaves from the internal walls, trailing carpet and bits of curtain.

The emergency services arrived quickly on the scene, swiftly followed by council officials and journalists. The lunch-time avengers of Fleet Street were quick on the draw and firing from the hip. Witnesses to the tragedy proliferated. The quotes grew lyrical. The *Daily Mirror* told its readers that there had been many escapes but none more remarkable than that of a man living on the fifteenth floor: as the floor collapsed beneath him he slid down to the ground on a slab of concrete. 'It is the most fantastic escape I have ever heard of,' said a fireman. 'He slid all the way down as if he was riding a magic carpet.' Among people watching the rescuers at work was a girl who claimed to have foreseen the flats' collapse. Schoolgirl Jackie Challis, fifteen, whose home was opposite Ronan Point, told of a 'terrible nightmare' she had had *thirteen* days ago. 'I dreamed the whole block had come down,' she said. 'I heard people screaming and saw others running for safety. It was horrible.

I told my schoolfriends and one or two people who live in the block but no one would listen to me.' Jackie's mother, Mrs Eileen Challis, said, 'I can remember her coming to me the next morning. She said that the block was going to collapse.' This barely credible story is interesting in retrospect; it demonstrates how easily history can be rewritten to fit the circumstances.

The trauma of the accident itself, and the subsequent herding together of Ronan Point residents by the media, had created, in effect, an artificial community. It was like an eerie premonition of the next generation's *EastEnders*, with all the dramatic irony and familiar characters. There was the old guy who had slept through the whole thing; firemen eventually smashed his door down, '. . . he came out in his pyjamas and said, "What the hell is going on?" ' On the same floor as Ivy Hodge, John Bruns was asleep in bed with his wife, Jean. Their baby, Samantha, eighteen months old, was in her cot nearby when the bedroom door shot off and flew across the room. John leapt out of bed and flung himself over the baby to protect her as the sound of falling masonry filled the room. Jean was expecting another baby next month. John and Jean thought their last moments had come. 'When the rumbling subsided,' he said, 'we tried to get out. Our front door and front wall had gone and I had to remove rubble with my hands to get to the staircase so we could escape.' They asked him what he did for a living. 'I'm a gas fitter,' he said. And then Ivy Hodge herself, swaddled and cheerful in her hospital bed, salt of the earth. In spite of serious injury, she looked very brave in her newspaper photograph.

By the time an emergency demolition squad started to remove the remaining floor slabs and other material, it was lunch time. Television crews were there to capture the block falling in dramatic monochrome. It dominated the weekend news reports. Families saw the images over and over again, saw Ronan Point falling. It was as if the very event had been captured on film. The first thing that I remember feeling was amazement that only one corner of the block had fallen down. It looked as though the whole block should have come down. In the pictures you could see the doors to other rooms in the flats, internal walls. We'd all been taught that industrialized building – construction using a kit of standar-dized, mass-produced parts – was a simple way to put things together, but behind those doors were people's living rooms.

I was in my second year of architectural studies at Aberdeen. I was playing in rock and roll bands and immersed in architectural theory and politics. At the same time there were French students picking up *pavoirs* and throwing them at the *gendarmes*. It was somehow part of it all. The collapse of industrial architecture was part of a general collapse of society itself. If this hadn't happened, some student would have blown it up anyway. A marriage of anar-chy and idealism would have massacred these buildings.

At architecture school we were still being taught industrialized building. Its structural systems had never, ever, been questioned. No one had ever suggested that it was dangerous in any way to live in a tower block. Suddenly there was a new idea that it was actually more dangerous to live above the ground than on it. There was a collective sigh of relief that it had happened so early in the morning.

People were suddenly using the rhetoric that had ushered in the era of post-war Britain. The golden age of the New Elizabethans was on the wane. Before the dust had settled around Ronan Point residents vowed they would never return to their former homes. The nation cheered them on. The tenants were seen as victims not of an explosion but of the flats they lived in. Why on earth should a high-rise block of flats be built to withstand an explosion? It had never occurred to anyone.

The 1960s, that elusive decade that began and ended with the Che Guevara T-shirt, crystallized in May 1968. The previous year had seen the summer of love; this year it was to be the summer of hate. Politicians were panicky enough before Ronan Point blew up in their faces. The housing programmes of the early 1960s had been the most rampant Britain had seen for a century. Government housing policy had inspired and cajoled; it had become tangible. And now it had become vulnerable, fragile. Paris was already out of control. London listened to the Rolling Stones singing 'Street Fighting Man' and waited.

The scene of the explosion drew a concerned visit from the

Home Secretary, James Callaghan. He later went to Number Ten, where he 'briefed' the Prime Minister, Harold Wilson. An immediate inquiry was ordered. On the BBC's *24 Hours* programme, Hubert Bennett, chief architect of the Greater London Council, said that if it were proved that the explosion had knocked out one of the concrete slabs, this type of construction might have to be looked at very seriously.

May 1968. The front page of the *Guardian* was classically bisected by a top-to-bottom picture of the collapsed Ronan Point flats. The proportions were perfect. The story itself was relegated to second lead. The main story had Pompidou calling on the French nation to reject anarchy. As he appealed for order, a convoy of riot police crossed Paris to head off thousands of students marching to join forces with workers on strike at the huge Renault factory at Boulogne Billancourt. He named Daniel Cohn-Bendit, the leader of a group of anarchist students known as the 'Enragés', as public enemy number one. More than 20,000 Renault workers at Le Mans, Flins and Cléon occupied the factories for an unlimited strike. Red flags were hoisted over the buildings, following the example of the Paris students in the Sorbonne.

Back in the East End of London, officialdom was as brittle as bureaucracy everywhere at the time; everyone knew that powerful social forces were stirring. There was now a struggle between the new and the moribund. While council officials who actually had to face the eighty families evacuated after the disaster met hostile and solid resistance to the idea that the tenants should return to their flats, those who were beyond a stone's throw tried to play the problem down. Mr Geoffrey Davies, Managing Director of Taylor Woodrow-Anglian, the company which had built the flats, was bullish. 'We have had a look at the block,' he said, 'and there is not the slightest indication that there is any structural failure.' Mr Davies told the *Guardian* that there would be no great technical difficulty about reconstructing the collapsed corner of the building. Asked if he thought people would be reluctant to move back, he replied, 'No, why should they?'

Meanwhile, the pound fell to its lowest level ever and Miss Elizabeth Taylor, the film actress, paid £127,083 for a diamond ring once owned by Vera Krupp, the late wife of the German armaments manufacturer. The highest American weekly death toll in the Vietnam war – 562 – was announced.

In the gymnasium at Hallesville Elementary School the Ronan Point residents sat huddled. The Ministry of Social Security set up an office to hand out emergency money, but an official said afterwards that he had received very few requests.

By the next week everyone had an opinion on Ronan Point. The issues raised were woven into the fabric of testy letters pages:

If it is found to be true that the Ronan Point flats explosion was caused by a gas leak, will the government or gas boards have second thoughts about charging for safety visits to suspected faults?

I had a gas fire fitted before Easter and found leaks in a number of places. After all this time I am still not able to use it. These days no one seems to take a pride in their job or think of the damage and inconvenience sloppy workmanship can cause.

The average contents of a box of matches openly printed on the label has steadily decreased in the last few years. Surely this concealed price increase should be a matter for the Prices and Incomes Board?

In the sombre aftermath of Ronan Point public opinion was beginning to congeal around the central premise that the boffins had botched it again. They split the atom and the next thing you know, two whole cities in Japan have been levelled. They send a monkey into space and the next thing you know, you've got non-stick saucepans and non-stick housing. With commendable hindsight, the media devoted themselves to new issues thrown up by new disciplines. The first and full flood of students emerging from polytechnics with degrees in sociology and finger painting had drained into the three most fertile fields: television, terrorism and politics. Some cells of glamorous Germans combined all three. In a spontaneous and uncharacteristic gust of affection for pop sociology the *Daily Mail* talked of the 'space-age neuroses' that befell families living high and poor in blocks of flats.

The collapse of a national architectural reputation mirrored the destruction of Ronan Point itself. Architecture had fallen like a pack of cards, but it had been the explosion of mass economy which had provided the impetus. Unaccustomed as they were to public speaking, architects scattered in the glare of publicity. They scrambled over each other in the race to get to the little bunkers. Once inside, however, they all aimed in the same direction: the National Building Agency, the Greater London Council, the Ministry of Housing and local government. That self-build architect of genius Walter Segal, who at the time of the collapse had won acclaim for building a house in Hampstead for just £800, said then, 'The culprits are the local authorities, particularly the Greater London Council and the National Building Agency. I think the NBA is especially responsible for this package dealing.'

A National Building Agency had been presented to parliament by the Ministry of Public Building and Works in December 1963:

There is an ever increasing demand for building, for both social and economic purposes. In the next ten years we must build millions of houses, many universities and colleges, schools, hospitals and other public buildings. We must also invest on a large scale in new factories, roads, power stations and port installations. To meet all these needs the output of the building industry must increase by more than 50 per cent in the next decade. This will have to be done without any great increase in the demand on the nation's limited labour resources.

Since the war the building industry has achieved notable increases in productivity. But if it is to cope with the upsurge of demand now facing it the industry will have rapidly to increase the industrialisation of its methods. In other words the industry must introduce more mechanisation and make greater use of factory-made components in order to achieve faster construction and to produce more than the skilled craftsmen available can build by traditional methods. This industrialisation of building presents special problems. The two obstacles which chiefly impede its growth are the lack of an assured and well-organised demand and the limited knowledge and experience of new techniques.

In the co-ordination of demand the building industry is dependent upon help from the clients for whom it works. It needs to be assured of orders which are large enough, and provide sufficient continuity of demand, to justify investment on a large enough scale for industrialisation. Of the total investment in new construction more than half is for public authorities. A special responsibility thus rests on public clients to organise their building demands into large contracts planned as far ahead as possible. If they discharge this responsibility adequately they will themselves be the chief beneficiaries: their buildings will be completed in time and at costs which are not inflated by labour shortages.

There were two main reasons for the creation of a National Building Agency. One was in the interests of consumers; the other was very much in the interest of producers, and did not appear in the White Paper.

First, the NBA offered to act as an impartial adviser on the selection of industrialized systems and their use. The Government had instituted a massive building programme, but without the necessary skill and knowledge needed to make intelligent decisions, how could local authorities decide? Those councils

which lack whole-time highly qualified professional staffs cannot be expected to evaluate and employ the new methods unless they have access to expert objective advice. Private clients and their professional advisers share this need for help in making informed judgments about the suitability of particular industrialised systems ... Because the industrialisation of building has developed so quickly in recent years there is a shortage of up-to-date knowledge about its techniques and possibilities. A new source of independent advice drawn from the available pool of specialised professional expertise appears to be essential.

And so it was. But just how diligent the NBA's 'evaluation' of the Larsen-Nielsen system* (the one for which the franchise had been bought by Taylor Woodrow-Anglian and used at Ronan Point) had been was to be revealed at the public inquiry. The *de facto* role of the NBA was as handmaiden to the large contractors, who were the key to success or failure in the race to build, for a race it certainly was. Richard Crossman, Housing Minister from 1964 until 1968, saw its role as more politically pragmatic and recorded in his *Diaries*: 'One difficulty was the split between us and the Ministry of Works, which controlled the NBA, the organisation which was designed to be a progress-chaser for the local authorities

---

* A large-panel building system, one of many proprietary systems used by local authorities. It was more economical than most to construct.

but which never for a moment did this job. When I got it transferred to our control I found it didn't do any better.'

It's easy to forget just how quickly things moved in the early years of the Wilson Government. From this distance the brutal equation (scale=achievement) looks uncomfortably like the national plans of Joseph Stalin in the post-war Soviet Union or, indeed, like the high-handed megalomania of President Ceausescu in present-day Romania. There was little time for analysis in the political laboratory that was social housing in 1960s Britain, a laboratory conceived of and constructed by the Conservative Governments of the 1950s and early 1960s and then taken over by the Labour Party. Under new management, the housing labora-tory was, in effect, ordered to give up any notions it might have about research and development and concentrate its mind on the more prosaic experiment of building in four dimensions: height, width, depth and time.

Architects are often asked why they went along with the notion that a better future lay in mass housing through the use of cheap building kits. One answer is that they were caught up in the same rush that swept everyone along in a mad dash for economic virility. Everyone, from Harold Wilson, with his photocall genius (there were public appearances with the Beatles, who received OBEs for their services to the export drive), to the five women from Surbiton whose 'I'm Backing Britain' campaign snowballed into a national obsession on the scale of a Comic Relief campaign (except that instead of wearing red noses, the faithful displayed thumbs up and Union Jacks). The articles of faith were progress and change, adapt or die. Because the monuments built to the mercurial new god of national planning endured – the unkempt tower block left isolated in a desert of unrealized landscaping and depopulated precincts – they became in the public imagination transformed from the effect to the cause of social haemorrhage. Ronan Point, like Richard Crossman – 'It took me fifteen months before I realised what was wrong' – was a speed victim.

7

Finding the Gaps

Returning from a trip to Liverpool in 1988, the Prince of Wales reported with some satisfaction that there was a useful future for tower blocks. Construction workers had dutifully informed him that crushed tower block mixed with soil makes an excellent amalgam for growing wild flowers. During the last decade, we have also learned that crushed architects make an excellent platform for public addresses on the state of the nation.

It is time to reassess the evidence. Tower blocks are not universally loathed. The good ones are good and the bad ones are bad, and the difference is how they are designed. Ronan Point was a failure not because architects were involved but because they were not.

While the facts central to the Ronan Point collapse have been largely forgotten, the referred blame has endured. Architects, once the heroes of the Festival of Britain, now stand accused of heinous crimes against the public estate; of creating high-rise hells, windswept piazzas, muggers' paradises. The clichés have passed into folklore, along with an image of the architect divorced from 'the people themselves'. In the foreground, a stark picture of the partially collapsed Ronan Point; in the distance, half-obscured by a cloud of opprobrium, the ruins of an ivory tower.

Architects had sounded warnings about high-rise buildings for years before Ronan Point. Traditionalists had always opposed them, while those architects who advocated industrialized building had, with some prescience, argued against penny-pinching. Tower blocks could be the robust and modern solution to housing shortages, but only if built with care and protected by aftercare. Doubts began to creep in early over the standard of quality control on site and the speed with which blocks were being constructed. There were successful alternatives to high rise – for example, Powell and

Moya's Churchill Gardens and Darbourne and Darke's Lillington Street, both for Westminster Council – but they had little impact on a government committed to large-scale renewal. The Treasury was paying the piper through direct subsidy and was therefore calling the tune. When Ronan Point came down, newspapers, politicians and the public lined up the professions and demanded to know which of them had a social conscience. Architects pulled on their hair shirts and stepped forward, articulating a concern for their part in the whole business. The architect, after all, was the captain of the building team. If the ship was going down, no prizes for guessing who was going down with it.

It is therefore somewhat ironic that it took an architect, Sam Webb, to co-ordinate the campaign which uncovered the truth about how Ronan Point was put together. In 1986, at the culmination of an eighteen-year struggle to get the local authority to open up the structure and investigate the suspect load-bearing wall joints, Webb's theory – that the joints, instead of being filled with dry-pack mortar, contained cigarette ends, tin cans, cement bags and fresh air – was finally vindicated. But it had been a long campaign, and a campaign led from the front by an architect. As part of the research for this book, I met Sam Webb in February 1989; the following account is based on that conversation.

Webb was part of a hugely influential generation of architects who had studied in the 1950s. He and others remember vividly an RIBA conference midway through the decade on high building. It had been orchestrated to coincide with a fresh legislative determination by the Conservative Government to crank the New Elizabethan age into life: a new housing act would increase the amount of subsidy for high-rise flats incrementally for each additional storey. Delegates were amazed to hear engineers of the calibre of Ove Arup tell the conference that the 11-inch cavity walls of a bungalow were 'much too strong'. Now engineers were talking about going up to fifteen or twenty storeys. Many people thought Arup was mad. On paper it seemed logical; in practice surely it was impossible. Everybody knew the kind of busking that went on during construction on a building site. Building isn't watchmaking.

In 1961 Webb teamed up with George Fairweather, a brilliant

architect who had worked with Joseph Emberton, arguably Britain's first practising modernist architect. Fairweather had done much of the design work for Emberton's highly praised Royal Corinthian Yacht Club, a seminal building which deployed glass and concrete in a way which either thrilled or appalled architects at the time. Like the apartment blocks Highpoint One and Two designed by the modernist practice Tecton, the building showed what modernism could do for the middle classes. The challenge was to bring that level of skill and technical application to mass housing. In fact, Emberton's practice had designed some early municipal housing – Brunswick Close, the heart of which was a group of three fourteen-storey tower blocks in Finsbury.

In the critical period of the early 1960s Webb, Fairweather, Walter Segal and a whole ghetto of architects, designers and writers lived in a gentle little enclave in Parliament Hill, north London, from where, on a clear day, you could see the flux of the capital city trembling under the fierce heat of reconstruction; tower cranes everywhere and flats rising among them, higher and higher. It was a fittingly brutal backdrop for architects and architectural students who were restructuring the ethos of education (in a more practical and technological way) as the urban fabric itself was being rebuilt. There was widespread rebellion against the stubborn principles of classicism. The hierarchical premise of classical architecture, which has always found favour with royalty, still had in the 1960s uncomfortably Germanic and totalitarian connotations.

In the 1950s an academic revolution was fomented by the Bartlett School of Architecture, whose home in Gower Street became a kind of seething tarwell of progressive thought. The Architectural Association school in nearby Bedford Square had been the centre of architectural theory and philosophy in the 1930s. Le Corbusier had visited in the 1950s, by which time it had moved on to the dawn of the Archigram group* and 'architecture without architects' – songs without words. It was left to the university school at the Bartlett to pursue the research.

* A group of architect–intellectuals who devised a system of pop graphics to articulate architectural polemic.

Emboldened by the new breed of architectural student who had been taken to see the Festival of Britain as a child and taught to regard buildings as monuments, Bartlett students went on strike and waged a war of attrition which removed the old guard, who took their pin-ups with them. On the bare studio walls where Palladian plans had once hung, up went the Pirelli calendars and diagrams of industrial components. In came crash courses in building economics; crypto-Stalinists jabbing their pipes at each other for hours on end at cocktail parties, arguing the relative merits of crawler and jib cranes.

The arguments were, indeed, largely academic. The new economic forces of politics and payola were well underway by the time architects were called in seriously to fashion new forms for these mysterious building systems. Those architects who sought to ask questions about system building were labelled reactionaries. What right had they to oppose the popular will? Just as the Prince of Wales has now marshalled a kind of alternative to apathy about the built environment – in the oven-ready 1980s it is easier to say, 'I agree with the Prince of Wales' than 'I don't know' – so the public of the early 1960s had its unsolicited champions, those who said, simply, that the means justified the end of slum clearance. Views which claimed to articulate a common will then, as now, were unimpeachable. Ordinary people reacted then as British people have always reacted to change: with an uncertain air of resignation. High-rise flats then, a giant out-of-town retail store on a greenfield site now. We say, 'Oh well, that's progress, I suppose . . .'

There was money to be made from system building, million upon million. By the time Ronan Point failed, Taylor Woodrow-Anglian had completed or was completing 6,000 homes, with contracts on the table for a further 4,000. It had two factories near Norwich and others at Northampton and Sunderland. TWA had been formed as an associated company to act as the franchise-holders for the Larsen and Nielsen system, which by 1968 had twenty-two licensees in twelve countries with a total yearly capacity of 22,000 homes. Originally introduced in Denmark in 1948 to 'improve building productivity, economize in the use of skilled

labour and contain rising prices', the system had as many versions
as there were subscriber countries.

With the exception of a few, architects discovered too late how
they fitted in the vast political machine that powered the born-
again construction industry. They were the cogs. The curriculum
for their training and education did not include politics, economic
manipulation or the Machiavellian machinations of mass housing.
After the RIBA's Oxford Conference in 1958, the profession produced its answer to the government call for architectural study to
move away from an apprenticeship system towards a more academic
formula.

A conference at the RIBA, the one at which Arup had evangelized about industrialized building, was a response to housing legislation which made building flats cheaper as they went higher.
It was the malleability, the flexibility of architects – a recurrent
professional trait – which undid them. Of course young architects
wanted to build big tower blocks in the East End, wanted to
consummate their academic love affair with buildings-as-monu-
ments, to create large and impressive structures. They always have,
from the Acropolis to St Pancras Station. The government wanted
large monuments, too, erected to the glory of their own housing
policies. Separate ideals found common theoretical and practical
expression in the tower block.

Young architects want to build 'big' now, in the new East End
of Docklands. It is a drive in any designer: to create, to build.
Masterplans and feasibility studies may be fascinating, but the
overriding aim is to leave something to posterity. And if the contemporary climate gives you the opportunity to fulfil that aim *and*
shelter people in new homes, the prospect is seductive. The welfare
state, of course, was itself still big in the 1960s before the money
ran out. The parallel wills of polarized governments had retooled
the construction industry. The idea of turning back, or even slowing
down, never entered the frame.

Unlike today, however, when architects, engineers, planners and
surveyors work increasingly as a multi-disciplinary team, the industry then was quite rigidly skill-segregated. The professional myster-
ies which separated architects from laymen also separated building

professionals from each other. If an engineer said the building would be structurally sound, that was that. It was his job. Sam Webb makes a fascinating analogy in his analysis of the period:

The government needed a major housing programme to stay in power; the buildings themselves became peripheral. Provided they could guarantee delivery and quantity, it was a case of 'never mind the quality feel the height'. The engineers said it could be done and the architects believed them. It's the same now with 1980s technology. A company buys a computer; spends a fortune on training a few people how to use it. If they leave, this big tin box sits in the corner with nobody knowing how to get the information out, so then they go back to a paper filing system. Curiosity gets the better of some, they open the computer, look inside and it's full of bullshit. That's how building systems were bought in the 1960s – on trust and in blind faith.

The image is compelling. Our practice bought an IBM word-processing system for the office from certified suppliers: six or seven terminals, about £50,000 worth of equipment. When the equipment needed servicing, we discovered the franchise had gone bust. We had to call in another agent, who opened up the boxes and found it full of non-IBM parts, just as Webb opened Ronan Point to find it full of the predicted rubbish.

There was circumstantial evidence at the time to indicate the kind of short cuts which facilitated the accelerating construction output. One former Architectural Association student remembers being part of a group of fourth-year diploma students taken to Morris Walk in Woolwich, the first Taylor Woodrow-Anglian scheme in London. The London County Council had placed a larger order for flats on the urging of the National Building Agency, whose recommendation secured the deal and allowed TWA to establish a factory in Norfolk. The AA students were taken along to see the first flats going up in the brave new world of Canning Town, where modern housing was rising at a rapid rate from the rubble of east London. The students had been taught system building theory and were brought along to see it in practice. It is alleged that as they arrived, one of the large wall panels was being lowered on to the two structural bolts and that it didn't fit. Then, says the student, they lifted it up, jiggered it around a bit; it still wasn't going to fit. A guy then ripped out all the polystyrene insulation, got a hammer and chisel and started knocking bits off. It still didn't fit. The foreman gave a signal like a judge to an executioner and this huge guy came along with a sledgehammer and smashed the bolts flat. The panel was slotted into place. We were aghast and challenged the foreman to explain his action. There was the sudden realization that we had been an audience to this appalling thing, the panel was hastily lifted off and we were ushered away.

It is Webb's view that the workmanship, as ever, was crucially important to the success or failure of high-rise blocks. The joints holding Ronan Point together had been designed in the 1940s by two Danish engineers. Like most system-building components, they were covered by patent and regarded as a commercial property. Despite the official Government line that research and development was being pooled by the National Building Agency – the NBA's Cleeve Barr told an audience in 1967 that the primary function of the agency, to appraise systems, had been made possible because 'there were in fact very few trade secrets in the technology of systems' – it was clear that the patents had been bought by the large contractors as an investment for the future. It was certainly in their interest to guard their systems against competitors' replicants for as long as possible. Detailed discussions between building contractor, architect and engineer started usually after the order had been placed and the timetable for construction agreed.

There are three central truths in the sad story of Ronan Point which have become blurred over the years. The first is that the building did not fall down. There was a gas explosion. The second is that the progressive collapse of the block's corner rooms would not have happened if the joints had been made properly. The third is that the architect's role was crucially limited: his job was to locate the block on the site, check that the daylight angles worked, maybe (if he was lucky) choose the finish of the concrete panels and select the flat plans from a pattern book.

The strength of the panels used at Ronan Point was actually extremely high, as Sam Webb will tell you. In terms of crushing strength, it was way beyond what was required by building regulations. And in theory, the 'continuous' joints used at Ronan Point should have spread the load uniformly through the structure. Every panel should have been identical in its structural integrity. But the designers wrongly assumed that the weight of the structure would overcome all forces, as happens, say, in a Gothic cathedral. This flawed assumption led them to reduce the thickness of the load-bearing wall panels down to only 6 inches (150 mm) and also leave out all the steel necessary to overcome bending forces. For once a building goes above five or six storeys, depending on the plan form, it wobbles. If the joints fail, each panel becomes a discontinuous, isolated component, you get bending moments throughout the building and it becomes much more vulnerable. Webb and other sceptical architects knew something was being missed out in the building process at the time the worst of the housing was going up. It was missing the vital ingredient – architecture – and no amount of politics or engineering could compensate.

Until Ronan Point happened, the public had not seen a system-building failure. When they did see it, all system building looked wrong. It is difficult to appreciate, half a century on from the Second World War, just how close London in the 1960s was to the the memory of large-scale damage. Nearly everyone knew what a bombed building looked like. A direct hit could reduce it to dust and rubble; an indirect hit could blast a hole in it. What was left, what survived, was ragged but looked solid. Ronan Point looked different, as if instead of resisting the force of the explosion it had simply given in.

The preliminary hearing into the Ronan Point incident opened at Newham Town Hall on 30 May 1968 in a climate of great bitterness as those with reputations to make or lose were drawn into the public arena. In addition to the four people who had died in the accident, another had subsequently died in hospital. The Ministry of Housing assured a sceptical public that it had been against high-rise buildings for years, citing some nebulous studies made by 'ministry sociologists'. Thomas North, Newham's chief architect, announced that seven new schemes for tower blocks in the borough had been cancelled on the drawing board, not, he maintained, because of adverse publicity following Ronan Point, but because of new housing-cost yardsticks to be introduced by the ministry the following January. With height no longer encouraged and subsidized, tower blocks would be more expensive in unit-cost terms than low rise.

In chief architects's offices all over the country, meanwhile, there was near panic. In London, which had been the logical mass testing ground for the National Housing Plan, the confusion was compounded by recent local government reorganization. Boroughs had been lumped together, and now vast paper storehouses contained tons of files on property owned jointly and severally by the previous councils. Technical officers and chief architects were on their hands and knees, scrabbling through the contents of plan chests.

Webb attended the inquiry when Fairweather gave evidence and quickly established himself as an expert witness on system building and the people involved, though an expert witness not for the official tribunal but for the unofficial investigations into corruption in local government that had now started.

The Ministry of Housing, before the end of the inquiry, ordered an immediate appraisal of all system buildings over six storeys and the cutting of gas supplies to any which clearly did not meet certain criteria of continuity in their joints between panels. The National Building Agency excused itself from listing those systems which might lack continuity because 'sponsors may occasionally have modified structural details themselves or have been asked to do so by clients'.

When the inquiry report came out in November 1968, it had some important things to say about the inadequacies of the building regulations and codes of practice, about the 'weak thinking' of the NBA and about the contractual arrangements for Ronan Point and its neighbouring blocks, whereby consulting engineers were appointed not by the building owner – the local authority – but by the contractor. Indeed, the consultancy was a subsidiary of the contractor. The report from the tribunal headed by Hugh Griffiths said it would be wrong to blame the designers of Ronan Point for their failure to foresee the possibility of progressive collapse; it had clearly been a blind spot for the whole industry. The code of practice relating to loading in buildings had been substantially unchanged by the British Standards Institution since 1952, when wind loading, for example, was calculated for a building stock largely in the two- to six-storey range. By 1968, many of the tower blocks going up were at least fourteen storeys high. Since 1952, responsibility for saying what was good building practice and what was bad had been steadily transferred from the bye-laws and regulations of the Ministry of Housing and local government to the codes of the BSI, a body advised solely by volunteers which had no statutory duty to initiate change or amend legislation.

None of this had the impact of the simple aside made in the report that: 'in the broadest sense it could be argued that the two major professions concerned – architects and structural engineers – have been found wanting, the former for their failure to call upon the latter, and the latter for failing to take much interest in system building generally.'

This was utterly wrong. Architects had consistently called on the expertise of engineers in the absence of adequate research findings or guidance, and engineers had led the crusade for industrialization in the 1950s. This allegation of professional dereliction of duty simply wasn't cricket. Having been bowled a nasty one, the *Architects' Journal* played an elegant stroke off the back foot, straight back down the wicket.

The report points to the false economy of cutting the volume of building research. This is the fault not, repeat NOT, of the professionals, who have always been calling for more research, but of the Government and of contractors, who together control the industry's purse strings. As a consequence of niggardliness the Government's advisers were tempted to think it safe to use Continental systems without first doing our own homework on them. It wasn't.

Nice try, but no cigar. The perception that the professions had somehow bamboozled everyone about system building took root in the public consciousness and has blossomed ever since. While the main plot of the moment was a stand-up fight between those who said it was dangerous to have gas supplied to suspect high blocks and those who said if buildings were not fit to have gas they were not fit to live in, the sub-text was that architects should have sorted it all out years before.

Meanwhile, *The Times* diligently sought the views of those Ronan Point tenants who had been rehoused in the neighbouring Merrit Point:

About a dozen families from Ronan Point who were involved in the disaster have demonstrated their confidence in high flats by moving in to the upper decks of Merrit Point. Nobody has refused to take a flat in the block, and a number of families said they were disappointed they could not get a flat in a higher storey because they had all gone. Yesterday the top storeys were noisy with the thumping of people moving in . . . the lace curtains and washing lines are going up in every balcony.

Were these the same people who had vowed never to return to Ronan Point?

The architectural profession has not been equivocal about high-rise buildings. Rather, since the 1950s, there have been those for and those against, as in any profession or indeed among people generally. And while tower blocks are now seen as suspect by the majority, there is plenty of evidence to suggest that many high-rise buildings, especially those which involved architects heavily from the word go, are perfectly safe, and more significantly, a worthwhile prospect for private developers to acquire and refurbish. And a shrewd investment for the owners, as desirable and appreciating homes.

The major architectural involvement at Ronan Point was that of Sam Webb, and he had nothing whatsoever to do with the design or construction of the building. His achievement was in getting Ronan Point pulled down once and for all. His brief was independent both of the building owner and the construction company. Webb responded to a plea for help from the residents themselves, who had become disenchanted with the tower block as it deteriorated steadily for twenty years. His expert guidance on how the tower-block community could become a force which would be impossible for Newham Council to ignore was the professional guidance of an architect.

Ronan Point collapsed not because architects were involved but because they were *not*.

The cheap end of system building, which proved fatally attractive to government and local authorities, was determined not by architects but by engineers. If architects had truly led the building programmes of the 1960s, instead of merely being shoved to the front to decide on the cladding and specify little more than the fixtures, high-rise urban living might today have been regarded as a success story. Unlike planners, whose job is to decide where the grey plains of mass concrete are to be dropped, or engineers, whose job is to make sure the structures erected upon them do not fall down, architects have to deal with the people who live there. The architect's art is to resolve problems of environment and shelter which are defined by people. Those architects who failed to do this in the 1960s are certainly to be criticized; those who were not given the chance should not be. When Webb came to be involved directly with the residents of Ronan Point, he was doing something which should have been done two decades earlier – that is, consulting the users.

We must remember that Ronan Point, for architects as much as anyone else, is a generation away. The number of architects practising today who were in practice at the time of Ronan Point's collapse is negligible. For the first time in the RIBA's history 40 per cent of the membership is under the age of forty. For how much longer must they suffer the consequences of the implied sins of their predecessors?

By the early 1970s Webb, through Labour MP Tom Driberg, was asking some awkward questions about significant omissions in the tribunal's evidence on Ronan Point. He made little headway. He was warned that repetition outside parliament of the accusations he was making about the construction of the tower block would render him liable to criminal libel.

Apart from sporadic visits to tenants, it wasn't until 1983 that Webb became the residents' own 'community architect'. After hearing him speak at a conference on the ageing of tower blocks, he was invited into one of the flats on Ronan Point, where he saw cracking around the joints and what appeared to be a gap at skirting-board level. He took a piece of paper, wrote the date on it and held it against the wall. When he let it go, it disappeared. The tenants asked him where it had gone. He told them – the flat below. 'They said, "What have you done?" I told them I'd just killed Ronan Point. I asked them if they could hear the television set from the flat upstairs. They said there was no one in the flat upstairs but that they could hear the television from the flat above that.' He took a couple of students with him on the next visit to survey the flats and talk to residents. Two floors below, Webb listened to the conversations: 'It was like the Whispering Gallery at St Paul's.'

In a very short time, Webb was being secretly consulted by tenants and some nervous structural engineers from boroughs all over London. 'There was one very bright engineer who had worked out that under certain loading conditions the whole front of this tower block could move sideways, because the wall joints and floor joints were in one single arrangement. He was quietly taken off looking at buildings and put on to drains and lifts.' Meanwhile, the tenants formed a network to pool their knowledge. Soon tenants from throughout England and Scotland were converging for workshops led by Webb to explain the principles of system building. Newham's housing committee chairman, Fred Jones, became an ally. He said publicly that the building should be emptied and tested to destruction. Consultants had produced a report for the council which said the flats were sound; Webb and the tenants said their own tests were more extensive, yet even they had not discovered a 36-lb liquid-gas container in one of the bedrooms – they had been denied access to the room because 'Granny was in there.'

The council suggested taking just one panel off one of the flats with the block still in occupation, though they were eventually persuaded of the public-relations risk involved. Webb's adopted community was increasingly worried about the risk of fire and what would happen to the building. Officially, it was the fear of accidental fire, but unofficially there were anxieties that tenants wanting to be rehoused might try to 'burn themselves out'. The contents of the joints were the key to structural integrity. Webb's theory that they were full of voids and rubbish was supported by residents' accounts of mysterious draughts. The tenants challenged Newham Council to conduct a full-scale fire test in Ronan Point to demonstrate the building was safe. In July 1984 the test was started and then dramatically stopped after just twelve minutes, because the floor slab over the fire room had deflected 69 mm downwards. One of the two precast units forming the slab was subsequently found to have split. The test, incredibly, was conducted in a third-floor flat which was thought by some to be risky – if that went, they said, the whole lot could come down. It was suggested later that that was as far as the fire hoses stretched.

Pressure on the council to open up one of the structural joints to see what was there became irresistible. Tenants, under Webb's guidance, knew exactly what questions to ask Newham to cause the maximum embarrassment and finally, in 1986, investigations revealed that all the key 'H2' joints contained less than half the specified dry-pack mortar. They were also packed with rubbish swept from the floor slabs during construction. Webb has very definite views on the question of whether government scientists overlooked the condition of the joints when they investigated the collapse in 1968 or were simply leaned on to say nothing.

Ronan Point was named after Harry Ronan, an east London Labour councillor who sat for years on the housing committee. His twenty-two storey municipal monument, which once stood so brazenly on the Freemasons Road estate, has gone.

The area is now being redeveloped with low-rise vernacular housing of the sort which draws approval from the highest quarters. A new housing scheme designed by architects Levitt Bernstein (for a private/public sector client and a market which demands a-cottage-in-the-country-in-the-city) sweeps away the remaining blocks bar one, Hume Point. This is to become a vertical community of nursing staff from the nearby general hospital, but the unpalatable twenty-three storey lozenge is to be given a spun-sugar coating: cylindrical corner towers and a cluster of pitched shed roofs on top, overclad in the aluminium skin which is now a familiar sight on the reformed characters of tower blocks born again in private ownership all over London. Actually, it doesn't look that bad,

especially when you know that if the lifts fail it is only junior
doctors and sprightly nurses – rather than exhausted mothers with
shopping and a baby in a pushchair – who will have to climb forty
flights of stairs.

After all this time, society has finally found a role for tower
blocks. These buildings are not good for housing families, unless
those families are close to the ground and have access to proper
gardens. Architects were saying this a quarter of a century ago.
But as the privatized tower blocks elsewhere in London – and Ray
Moxley's new belvedere tower at Chelsea Harbour, a significant
return to the idea of a landmark building – have proved, high-rise
blocks are excellent for young childless couples and single people
who need little space, have no time for gardening and welcome
the chance of a breathtaking view. If families have to be housed in
high-density warrens, they each need their own burrow and part
of the earth they can call their own. All young single people need
is a nest.

We must look very closely at those tower blocks remaining in
local authority ownership, as closely as Sam Webb looked at Ronan
Point. If, for example, the two towers built to the same system on
the Broadwater Farm estate have the same defects of construction,
they must be pulled down. Others which are demonstrably sound
of structure should be rehabilitated and used to house people
without children – an area of the market which is chronically short
of suitable housing and has grown more desperate as our cities
have seen an exodus of the middle aged to the suburbs and a
flood of young people coming into town, looking for work and the
stimulation of urban life.

Between 1971 and 1981 the total number of households in Great
Britain increased by about 6.5 per cent. The population increase
was less than 1 per cent. There were marked discrepancies within
household types and an intensification of trends through the 1970s:
one-person households increased from 17 per cent of all households in 1971 to 25 per cent in 1984, while the proportion of
households with dependent children declined over the same period
from 39 to 33 per cent.

It would be as foolish to disregard the logical link between savable tower blocks and one-person households as it was foolish for housing authorities in the 1960s to imagine families living 200 feet above the ground.

Good riddance to Ronan Point and all other jerry-built housing. Ronan Point itself is now dead and buried, though not, as perhaps the Prince of Wales would have wished, under a meadow of wild flowers. Taylor Woodrow-Anglian sold the building to contractors before it was finally dismantled and broken up. But then they bought it back again: they landed a major construction job in Docklands and needed hardcore. Ronan Point is now under the runway of the Docklands City Airport.

8

Noun to Verb

The architectural profession has worn the ball and chain of high-rise housing for the last twenty years. We were sentenced to death by association for the errors of industrialized building. This was commuted to a kind of exile from public credibility; we joined the social workers and used-car salesmen.

But we were framed. Architects had grave misgivings about high-rise housing before and during its construction. They also had grave misgivings afterwards, but these were quite rightly dismissed as 20/20 hindsight. Our critics will say that the buildings did not design themselves, that the architect determined the forms of tower blocks and was pleased so to do as it furnished an opportunity for egomania on a grand scale: 'My tower block's bigger than your tower block.' There is some truth in all of this; there were undoubtedly architects who welcomed the chance to build tall. The modern movement had urged a programmatic break with tradition. Tower blocks certainly did that. But the forces which put this opportunity on the drawing board had nothing to do with architecture. It was construction without aspiration: we were building high because it was fast and (in theory) cheap and there was political gain involved. To what extent, in truth, can you 'design' a building which, you are told, has to be twenty-two storeys high, must use a proprietory system which has been bought blind by the local authority last week and for which all main relevant dimensions are predetermined?

High-rise housing was put up by politicians and let down by builders. For every architect who supported the initial wave of large-scale high-rise programmes, there were many who knew that the dream of a society which could be reformed by bold strokes of visionary genius had been betrayed. Any lingering hope that there would be time to ask questions later was quickly dispelled. The lambs of 1950s high rise – Lasdun's fourteen-storey cluster blocks in Bethnal Green sprang from his imagination even as he was working on a two-storey primary school in Paddington – these exquisite, tottering lambs, had lost their way and were lonely, bleating. And the next generation of lambs was heading where most little lambs have always gone.

Municipal high-rise housing was modernism's slaughterhouse. It plucked a Corbusian apartment block, floating white and serene in a verdant Continental suburbia, and brought it to England. Of course, it couldn't be the same. The sky, instead of being a perpetual azure, was the colour of beaten lead. The landscaped public lawns and gardens, alive with the urbane chatter of people who looked like Stephane Audran and Jean-Louis Trintignant, became building sites full of 'dour-faced men dressed in a variety of old suede shoes and too large lounge suits', as Alison and Peter Smithson, the husband and wife team who pioneered British Modernism in its 'New Brutalism' phase, so glumly informed us. A bourgeois dream of egality had plunged downmarket faster than stripped pine. The beautiful textures and finishes of Le Corbusier's *Unité d'habitation* at Marseilles had thrilled an entire generation into believing that this was the future of housing. A porridge of rough concrete cast in formwork of coarse-grained timber was conjured, under the Eastmancolor Mediterranean sky, into a people's palace. Beauty and the Beast, the detailing and the scale. Never mind designing it, just let me live there! The mountains, the woodlands, the sea, the 2Cvs everywhere, full of nut-brown tennis players in black wraparounds, the warm wine and the nice crusty bread. This was not the Walworth Road, however. By the time the urge for mass housing could no longer be ignored, the form had turned to formula and the *ville radieuse* had become tower blocks inside a ring road. In place of singular craftsmanship there was sandwich panel slotted into sandwich panel; no frills, no complexity, just mass housing at its lowest common denominator. It was the difference between looking at the pictures in a holiday brochure and looking out of the window.

Even hardliners like the Smithsons – who, with other modern architects, urged us to take up the Corbusian challenge to fashion moving relationships from brute materials – even the brutalists, had warned against building high tower blocks in the idiosyncratic urban grain of Britain. In 'Criteria for Mass Housing' the endlessly revised 'manifesto' devised by the Smithsons for Team X in 1957, they posed some awkward questions for designers of tower blocks: 'Is the scale of the unit related to the size of the parent community? . . . can November 5 be celebrated? . . . Is there something worth looking at out of every dwelling?'

They identified sources of anxiety in flats:

The house does not actually belong to the inhabitant, engendering insecurity and lack of pride in ownership . . . Responsibility for upkeep ambiguous . . . Heights above the ground arbitrary (they are 'rational' only in the sense that they are an additive of the minimum byelaw requirements). There is no expression in the means of access, construction, or the flat type that there is any difference of altitude, or indeed that one has left the ground at all . . . No real place for children to go and play . . . No human reason for being raised in the air, no tangible gain from being lifted off the ground . . . Lack of choice . . . The relationship of family life lifted up in the air to the rest of the town or city has not been considered . . . If the development answers only byelaw and health standards and is consequently like barracks of filing cabinets, it can be as soul-destroying as slums and similarly without hope.

This was being said by architects thirty years before the Prince of Wales's *Vision of Britain* was shown.

It is a tribute to the local authorities' effective system of blame dispersal that, after Ronan Point, architects were perceived as the professionals whose concern began and ended with the built form, while the councils were acting in the best interests of their tenants. In fact, the reverse was true. Architects throughout the 1960s consistently argued for more time and more money to evolve new ways of bringing communities together in an urban context; the architect's unit of calculation was the family. What did it need and how could this be achieved? The local authorities, meanwhile, were consumed with the problems of building economics; their unit of calculation was the 'dwelling'. How cheaply could it be made, how many of them could you stack on top and how quickly?

The word 'house' became a class indicator and changed from noun to verb.

As the level of 'dwelling construction' notched upwards in the mid-1960s – 200,000 a year and rising – the clamour from architects grew. We accept the need for high-density housing in cities, they said; what we do not accept is that this has to be high rise. The architects pointed to high-density low-rise schemes and told the local authorities that these could achieve the same densities *and* keep families on the ground *and* create better communal space. The authorities smiled and nodded, but kept looking at their watch – they had a deadline to meet. It was already too late to discuss the fundamental social question: if you are to group people in housing, how large should the groups be? There was no socially meaningful unit bigger than the individual family. Social housing had to derive its meaning from its architectural – its 'plastic' – form.

Walter Segal, whose no-nonsense methods of self-build housing were to become a symbol for 'community architecture' long before its time, predicted the failure of high tower blocks as they were being built. They failed on two counts, he argued. First, a modernist form of visual accentuation had been appropriated and used as the norm: tower blocks were not sited to alleviate the urban landscape but thrown down in clumps, determining a new scale of living wholly inappropriate to uncomprehending Britain. Second, if tower blocks were discredited, the opportunities they opened up for targeted social housing would be frittered away. Architects recognized that tower blocks could provide both strong urban landmarks and excellent housing for, say, the young, single flat-dweller. But the urgent need was for humane family housing.

There was not merely a theoretical basis for the scepticism about high-rise housing. In several seminal schemes architects had demonstrated in practice how people could be housed in a civilized environment, and to densities which satisfied the programmes of housing authorities. While the London County Council had, in 1955, used the construction of an estate at Camberwell in south London to explore the budget implications of 'systematic design' with a tower crane, kit parts and poured-concrete cross-walls, architects like Powell and Moya and Darbourne and Darke were working on principles that started with the people who would live in their schemes. Powell and Moya's Churchill Gardens, completed in 1950 and built for Westminster Council, demonstrated a careful and masterly interpretation of the pragamatic school of European modernism. The estate was cool and light, set in parallel blocks, low and high, and executed in glass and steel and concrete.

Like Churchill Gardens, Lillington Street was the result of a Westminster Council architectural competition. It was won by the young team of John Darbourne and Geoffrey Darke in 1961. The two had been friends before Darbourne left to study for his Masters degree at Harvard. The Lillington Street scheme formed the basis of his thesis. He won the competition, rang Darke from Los Angeles and suggested a partnership. Darke agreed. The first of three building phases started in 1964; phase three was completed in 1972. The evolution of the design and its response to the needs of the people whose homes were being created took place against the backdrop of the rise and fall of the tower block. Its success shows the crucial importance not only of architectural ingenuity but of client responsibility. The local authority appointed Philip Powell as architectural assessor for the Lillington competition and backed the selection of the scheme with a £1.3 million budget for the first phase – 244 flats and maisonettes – which was generous by any housing-authority standards. The scheme not only diverged from Powell's Churchill Gardens, with its slabs and open parkland, but from several of the other competition entries, which featured twenty-five-storey tower blocks. Darbourne and Darke had proposed not a housing estate but an homogeneous environment, with blocks linked by 'roof streets' and walkways and punctuated with courtyard spaces, play areas, planting and landscaping. The construction was to be of brick cross-wall and would be faced in brick, taking its cue from a surviving Victorian church at the centre of the site. Although the highest deck access blocks were eight storeys high, most were around four or five, echoing the surrounding residential area of Pimlico.

And it was housing people at a density of 218 bed spaces per acre, pushing the urban limits set by the Ministry of Housing and local government to the maximum, and then some. By the time phase three was under way, housing-cost yardsticks had been introduced, a measure which reduced the cost of mass housing in the short term only. For how could anyone truly say they were spending *too much* on social housing?

The architects were kept to a tight schedule, but were not bullied into cutting corners or rushing the job.

While compulsory-purchase orders were being assembled, the young Drake and younger Darbourne (thirty and twenty-six years old respectively) were engaged by Westminster to survey, measure and assess the site. This was, literally, grassroots work from the bottom up. They were able to spend their professional time at a critical point in the building process – the start. They used their training and creative skills to understand the site through a process of architectural phrenology. They later allowed themselves a small glow of satisfaction when their survey calculations 'closed' to within a margin of error thought unachievable by any but the swarm of surveyors then to be seen all over London, measuring it as if for the undertakers.

The architects expanded the brief to include a new section which would integrate flats for the infirm with the more ambulant pensioners on the scheme. Set among the roar of traffic and hemmed in by existing residential development, Lillington Street set out to create a quiet environment on a human scale and yet to continue a London tradition of dynamic density: the original Victorian four-storey houses on the site had a density far in excess of 1960s levels. The objective was to continue the tradition of green squares linked in a London landscape while exploring new complexities of scale and space in which a modern population could live together.

The structural premise was a standard 9-inch brick cross-wall; the whole scheme was also faced in brick. The trouble taken to find just the right type of brick illustrates the painstaking care with which the project was determined. The architects wanted a brick that matched that used in G. E. Street's church of St James-the-Less – the only historic reference on the site. None could be found, despite a long search. The anxieties of the clients, who were keen to get on with 'a brick' if not 'the brick', were skilfully negotiated and – out of the blue – the architects stumbled upon an old man called Mr Cornish who had just bought a brickworks near Hastings, having moved from Essex. Mr Cornish made Essex bricks the Sussex way, and with exactly the glow of bronze the architects were looking for, by hand in a kiln he stoked himself. They had to stockpile for nine months before building.

Phase one of Lillington Street was handed over amid widespread acclaim. It won an RIBA regional award as the unanimous choice from fifty-two entries:

The layout has a pleasant domestic and informal scale, a most impressive achievement with the need to squeeze so many people into the site. Blocks are more reminiscent of the college campus than of municipal tenements. Elevated streets, worlds removed from traditional municipal access balconies, are wide and friendly, sheltered from noise and luxuriant with planting – yet another example of the care for human needs.

Phase two was developed along similar lines, a series of interlocked internal and external spaces, sheltered and open.

It may all seem straightforward today, but at the time Lillington Street was being developed, those of us at architecture school were being taught the Radburn method of pedestrian and traffic segregation, blocks of houses set formally in a gridded geometry. At Pimlico, the cars were out of sight and the spaces around the homes were for people. While we were doing layouts of main roads, feeder roads, footpaths and so on, Lillington Street broke all the doctrinaire rules of a relentless building system. It allowed itself to be shaped by the nuances of the site itself and deployed the 'complexity and contradiction' preached by Robert Venturi which said that if God wasn't in the details he was certainly in the idiosyncrasies of a scheme.

Lillington Street had used standard components in a highly individualistic way. No other inner-city housing scheme in this country had used bricks in any number since the war; and nobody, thanks to the variables of Mr Cornish's firing process – he burnt to just the right degree the ones used for copings – had used *this* brick.

A rash of housing schemes in the period shortly after Lillington borrowed not its architectural thesis that individual schemes deserve individual solutions but its brick – or an approximation of it. Stylistic echoes of the brick facings and stained windows of Lillington appeared later in less well-thought-out developments.

To the brutalists, the scheme would have appeared to be taking the easy way out, ignoring the possibilities that raw concrete, say, could have afforded and opting for that most traditional of mass components, the brick. It was a cultural security blanket, a tangible link with the past, hand-sized, understandable and infinitely flexible. The more progressively minded commentators were partially reassured by the use of flat roofs.

When part of Ronan Point came down in 1968, phase three of Lillington Street was going up. Its final form was to reflect the crucial aspect of the relationship between client, architect and user which had formed so successful an experiment. During phase two the architects became aware of shortcomings in the layout. They were learning by doing. Although the space had been maximized to allow as large a public area as possible, the architects developed a strong awareness of the need for families to be housed at ground level. And although the wide terraces and split-level access decks of the earlier phases provided playing-out areas and individual planted borders, the demand was still for gardens.

If this had seemed out of the question in 1961, when the density planned for phase one had been 218 people to the acre, it was surely impossible now. High-density housing was expensive, and phase three was even denser – 254 to the acre. Added to that was the imposition of the housing-cost yardstick, which pared down the budget to sobering levels. On phase one it had cost £1,357 to house each person on the estate; phase three reduced the unit spend to £1,144. The architects argued, successfully, for the original brief to be torn up and to be allowed to redesign. The result was a multi-level solution which put families with young children in ground-floor maisonettes or those with ground-floor access. By importing soil, small gardens were created, sometimes over garages but all with a private gate and a definable perimeter. Mass housing had come home.

9

Unfinished Symphony

What the visitor will see on the South Bank is an attempt at something new in exhibitions – a series of sequences of things to look at, arranged in a particular order so as to tell one continuous interwoven story. The order is important. For the South Bank Exhibition is neither a museum of British culture or a trade show of British wares; it tells the story of British contributions to world civilisation in the arts of peace. That story has a beginning, a middle, and an end – even if that end consists of nothing more final than fingerposts into the future.

Festival of Britain Guide, 1951, 2s 6d

'Banks 1 m (3 ft 3 in) high provide permanent basis for approved hedge planting.'

A Design Guide for Residential Areas, County Council of Essex, 1973, £4.50

The rugged optimism which characterized the Festival of Britain in 1951 was inspired less by faith in the future than by a suspension of disbelief in the present.

Like Powell and Moya's Skylon, it was said, Britain had no means of visible support. The economy was in tatters; there was austerity and rationing.

The unfinished symphony that was the Festival of Britain was composed by architects relying on a generous and unwavering patron (£11 million for an 'off the ration' fling!). For a nation that had wearied of war and had now flooded the carburettor with peace-time ennui, the suspense was killing.

Everybody wanted a peace to end all wars. All hope was in a future which was comfortingly technological and authoritative. A world, too, in which lesser nations looked to Britain – now shorn of colonies and empire – as democracy's residuary body. The Cold War was just, well, warming up. Britain had been pensioned off

by the new world powers, for whom the Second World War had
been a coming of age. The Festival of Britain was the gold watch
we awarded ourselves. We had our memories, of course: the Raj,
the white man's burden, the eternal referee and champion of fair
play and support for the underdog. Our future was at home now,
not abroad. We had retired.

The year of the Festival of Britain was the *annus mirabilis* in
which the seminal science-fiction film *The Day the Earth Stood Still*
was released. It was sensational and retains, to this day, a freshness
of vision that the Festival echoed. The panicking Earthlings – the
ones who shrieked and fainted and the ones who wore tin hats and
wanted to nuke the spacecraft – were all American. But the mes-
sianic alien whom bullets could not kill was English: Michael
Rennie. There was something so *right* about this interplanetary
harbinger speaking with the suave command of the officer's mess
('The universe grows smaller every day . . .'). The idea that an
extra-terrestrial power would invigilate over a world on probation
and reduce it to cinders should nation not speak unto nation, as it
had been instructed to do by the BBC, had both a timeless and
timely appeal. Britain was no spring chicken, but it could still bang
together the heads of Uncle Sam and Ivan the Ruskie. Delusions
of grandeur were never more poignant. Imperial memories and a
yearning for a new, shimmering future – what we wanted was a
resurrected Lord Reith in a spaceship.

For architects, the drawing in of our borders occasioned little
regret. The task ahead was thrown into sharp relief by this new
national introspection. Build, build, build. The best for our people;
the new sciences and the new arts could be yoked and harnessed.
And the Festival of Britain suddenly changed the public's perception of architects, too. Previously they had been widely regarded
with suspicion; they were airy-fairy shirtlifters with wispy beards
who wore clothes like those oily little *Cherman* spies in the B
movies. Now it was apparent that some of them were human after
all. Better than that, they were fun to have around, the life and
soul of the party. Young couples waltzed outside Ralph Tubb's
Dome of Discovery to the sound of Joe Loss or strolled beneath the
magical Skylon, and the architect was transformed into a popular

romantic hero, a *Woman's Own* idol, with his untipped cigarettes, sports jacket with leather patches at the elbows and a racy foreign car.

If that elusive period 'post-war Britain' started anywhere, it started with the Festival. It now stands as an historical curiosity, an overture, a celebratory, anthemic set piece which has endured in the nation's affection as Handel's anthems have endured. The fact was that the architecture of the Festival was derivative, a summation of design innovations that had been kicking around Europe for some time. The tensile structures on the South Bank – the suspension cables and the light, airy feel of wafer-thin materials floating in space – bore a remarkable resemblence to Renzo Zavanella's work at the Milan Fair of 1948.

The 'live architecture' exhibition at Lansbury in Poplar, on the other hand, demonstrated just how conservative a vision of the future could be. Thirty acres of bomb-scarred land on the fringe of what is now London Docklands was designated as the site for a practical counterpoint to the riot of theory on the South Bank. A residential neighbourhood was built to the designs of a committee of architects. It included a market and the country's first shopping precinct. And, like the first cuckoo of spring, the unfamiliar silhouette of a tower crane appeared on the site as the shape of things to come. Despite its enormous significance in terms of building to a human scale and offering a welcome alternative to the drab surroundings of ravaged, temporary London, the Lansbury site inevitably lacked the thrill of the boldly orchestrated South Bank. For, while the Dome and the Skylon explored newness, Lansbury was still rooted in the cultural continuum of the vernacular, which was by the 1970s to celebrate its triumph in the Essex *Design Guide*.

At Lansbury, the London County Council planning brief set the parameters:

The buildings, of varying heights, will be grouped round closes and spaces of different sizes, each with its individual character. In some cases there will be children's playgrounds in the centre of blocks, completely protected from traffic. The layout is in fact a series of neighbourly groups linked together by open spaces. While this type of layout is new to the East End of London and the contrast between new and old forms of development is likely to prove striking, the architectural treatment of most of the build-ings will include the use of London stock bricks and purple grey slates which are traditional building materials for this part of Poplar.

The brave new world was to have a pitched roof.

The more rigorously 'modern' examples of Festival architecture merely legitimized the pale imitations which were to follow. Sir Misha Black, one of the Festival's co-ordinating architects, said in 1975 in an interview with Mary Banham and Bevis Hillier, that

it suddenly proved that Modern architecture with a capital M was in fact acceptable . . . after the South Bank, [property speculators] realized that this kind of architecture was common currency, that people accepted the South Bank without cavil. And it released the worst kind of bastardized modern architecture which the country had ever seen, and from which we have been suffering ever since.

The Festival had indeed been a tonic to the nation, as its protag-onists had claimed: but after it had been dismantled, government and the local authorities realized that some of the ingredients – architectural skill in particular – were expensive. The tonic became a patent medicine, administered in huge quantities to an ailing environment in the form of system building. It made us feel worse, and helped provoke the nostalgic yearnings which turned aspiration away from the future and back to the past. The 'fingerposts to the future' set up by the South Bank visionaries became traffic signs saying 'major road ahead' and 'multi-storey car park'.

The green fuse of reforming zeal had driven visionaries forward since William Morris. His sentimental brand of socialism, however, seemed hopelessly outdated to a world picking up the pieces left scattered by the Second World War, seemed effete and tentative in a traumatized Britain. What did Victorian philanthropists (inno-cent of the atom bomb, television, modernism) have to offer? The answer, as it turned out, was the blueprint for suburbia. While the Festival of Britain offered a way of life which was technological and cosmopolitan, its antithesis was a uniform vernacular, enshrined two decades later in the Essex *Design Guide* of 1973. The idea that you codify what you imagine people want and then

call it civilization was promulgated, among others, by William
Morris in 1874:

Suppose people lived in little communities among gardens and green
fields, so that you could be in the country in five minutes' walk and had
few wants, almost no furniture for instance, and no servants, and studied
the (difficult) arts of enjoying life, and finding out what they really wanted:
then I think that one might hope civilization had really begun.

As city centres in the 1960s contracted within the grip of ring
roads and office development, the suburbs expanded. The Festival
premise that the city could be an exciting place to live had withered.
The city was a miserable place to live, the familiar patterns
destroyed and replaced with cheap imported housing and over-
powering office blocks, which imposed a new uniformity. London's
urban escapees sought refuge in the overspill sanctuary of the
Home Counties, in particular Essex, whose border with the East
End had become more and more blurred since the war. Piecemeal
development of new housing in the county appeared to local planners in the late 1960s, though, to be out of control and out of
sympathy.

If the Festival had marked the beginning of post-war Britain,
the Essex *Design Guide* marked the end. In a prescriptive move
which was to have far-reaching consequences, Essex county planning department published, in 1973, its *Design Guide for Residential
Areas*, which sought to introduce a vernacular code which would
act as a regulator for suburban living. Housing would conform to
a kind of architectural dress code: traditional materials, pitched
roofs and a formulated layout. It was rigorously imposed and created a new uniformity based on past principles, a new theme
retrospectively conjured from old variations. It had little to do with
the modern world, save for the key role Essex played in stimulating
the growth of estate agencies. By the 1980s the reassuring swathe
of neo-vernacular houses stretched, and yawned, from Gants Hill
to Colchester.

When the Prince of Wales attacks the 'look' of towns and cities
ravaged by development in the 1960s, he is criticizing the mistakes
of planning and highway engineering. His speech to City planners

at the Mansion House in 1987 was directly inspired by architectural writers Colin Amery and Dan Cruickshank, whose book *The Rape of Britain* has been a conservationist's gazetteer since its publication in 1975, European Architectural Heritage Year. In a series of shockingly juxtaposed 'before' and 'after' photographs, the town planning excesses suffered by historic towns from Truro to Aberdeen were catalogued. Page after page; brainless, heartless developments. The anthology was introduced by John Betjeman, followed by stark pictures of Ballance Street in Bath, a perfect composition of Georgian buildings going higgledy-piggledy up the hill like a Beatrix Potter narrative. Below this tranquil scene was another picture: apocalypse now, the same view – could it be the same? – all changed, swept away for council housing of the stalag persuasion.

It was a travesty, this innocence so brutally shattered. But who said a new road and a council estate should go there in the first place? Planners and highway engineers. Architects may have put their foot in it, but the footprint was there already; their steps followed the chalk marks like novices at a dance studio.

The weapons of urban destruction, said Amery and Cruickshank, formed a mighty arsenal: money, mediocrity, concrete ('concrete is a joyless material, it is universal and it bears no more relationship to Aberdeen than to Addis Ababa') and the Comprehensive Development Area. The CDA represented a major tranche of post-war planning legislation, and it allowed local authorities the power not just to withhold planning consent but to implement large-scale clearance and development themselves by exercising an early form of right-to-buy called compulsory purchase. An inconveniently sited terrace street could now be *bought* out of the way.

This process was planning, not architecture. The climate had changed since the Festival of Britain, and the species of liberal progressive architect included in Michael Frayn's definition quoted in *A Tonic to the Nation* – 'the radical middle classes, the do-gooders; the readers of the *News Chronicle*, the *Guardian* and the *Observer*; the signers of petitions; the backbone of the BBC. In short, the herbivores' – had become extinct, or at least kept out of the way as the new carnivores of planning scavenged on the concrete savannah. At about the same time as popular music started to be created by producers instead of musicians, urban layouts moved from architectural masterplan to planning committee. A new equation was introduced. The solution was to be Jerusalem, as ever; the variables, architecture and people, were replaced by planning and cars. New roads cut through people's towns like an axe through wedding cake; transport engineers built vast link roads and interchanges which resembled Lubetkin's Penguin Pool on an hallucinogenic scale.

Post-war Britain had started with high hopes of a new society planned by design. Instead, we have landed ourselves with the spreading *embonpoint* of a suburbia designed by planning. The Essex *Design Guide* is longhand for 'whatever the planners say'; and they spoke in unison. It is hardly credible in retrospect that the *Design Guide*, which made mandatory a filtrated vernacular style composed from compulsory 'local' elements, was offered as an antidote – as was claimed in the introduction – to housing which 'has a dreary suburban uniformity and lacks any specific Essex characteristics'. It managed to be both small-minded and high-handed at the same time. Defying uniformity with the conviction of an initiate, the team led by planners from the county council laid down the law:

In the following sections words like *satisfactorily enclosing space* and *well designed* will frequently be used. It might be thought these words imply an opinion; that one informed person might regard something as well designed and that another would not. This is not the case; with all aspects of design there are well-proven principles to be observed.

It went on to articulate the theories of formal and informal Arcadia. The first version had straight roads with the houses hidden by trees, the second was based on a picturesque theory, popular with owners of country house parks, in which meandering walks (now winding roads) 'are designed to allow the "villas" to appear at intervals as the surprise features in the landscape'.

For 'villas' read 'chalet bungalows'. The genteel self-righteousness of suburbia pretending it isn't allows any kind of abomination in the name of freedom of choice, then makes it respectable with the imposition of a standard roofscape and approved layouts. The

eerie South Woodham Ferrers in Essex, a controlled experiment
in creating a dormitory town from an existing hamlet, even has a
mock village centre; it mocks the new settlement from an isolated
greenfield site. On closer inspection, the traditional materials and
Design Guide roofs are found to be camouflaging an Asda supermar-
ket with attendant phoney clock tower.

The success of the Essex *Design Guide* was not confined to that
county. Other planning authorities were impressed by the way
helpful guidelines could be invested with the force of law. Vernacular as a formula for designing and building out of town gathered
momentum rapidly during the 1970s. It was settling for less, settling
for a consensus which was acceptable to the largest number of
planners and developers. For this was the key.

At the front of the Essex *Design Guide* is a Foreword signed by
Geoffrey Rippon, Secretary of State for the Environment:

By putting forward a clear and constructive statement of their policy
for general guidance, the Essex County Council have made a bold and
imaginative move to establish a firm basis of understanding between would-
be developers and the committees and officials having responsibility for
measures of control. All must surely gain real benefit from the initiative
which could, I believe, reduce the time now required for the developer to
obtain permission and, hopefully, the number of appeals against the refusal
of permission.

At the end is a list of bodies thanked for their comments and
assistance. At the top of the list is the Aluminium Window
Association.

The swerve back to vernacular was a conscious move, promoted
by planners who had seen the urban vision of redevelopment curdle
under their gaze. The city was unpopular as both a planning
concept and as a place to live at the time the *Design Guide* was
published. We are now far enough away from the rural/suburban
movement to know that it succeeded where the urban movement
of the 1960s failed simply because it aimed so much lower.

Vernacular used to mean native, or indigenous, or local, or
endemic. But vernacular in the planning sense has an opposite
meaning. For the need to set a style of building was occasioned

not by natives wanting to rebuild their homes but by newcomers wanting new ones. The vernacular which has spread its influence across the country is not endemic at all; it is epidemic. It is no longer about how buildings looked before the war but about how the one built a fortnight ago down the road looks.

The last half of the twentieth century opened, for Britain, with a national festival. The century will close with one. Halfway through this period, neo-vernacular design was at its most potent. The Prince of Wales's defence of vernacular design is a rearguard action, for the allure of Europe and the millennium is starting to stir us from hibernation again and focus our imagination on the sort of place we want our new king to rule over, after the next Festival of Britain.

10

That'll Do Nicely

Section 52 of the 1971 Town and Country Planning Act allows local authorities to exact a kind of community levy on new development (the italics are mine):

A local planning authority may enter into an agreement with any person interested in land in their area for the purpose of restricting or regulating the development or use of the land, either permanently or during such period as may be prescribed by the agreement; and any such agreement may contain such incidental and consequential provisions (*including provisions of a financial character*) as appear to the local planning authority to be necessary or *expedient* for the purposes of the agreement.

The aim, ostensibly, had been to secure the necessary hidden agenda from developers in terms of environmental improvements or a financial contribution towards them. It was only fair; give and take. In the heart-stopping world of fast-track development, however, the difference between a gift to the local community for allowing you to maul their neighbourhood and a straightforward cash bribe offered to the local authority is so thin it is transparent. I remember a cartoon by architectural wit Louis Hellman showing a borough council planning committee in session. The chairman introduces the next application, for luxury flats, which is pinned up and hidden from our view. The developers are Preystalk Properties plc. The committee members are enthusiastic: 'Ah, yes, this is a most impressive proposal' . . . 'I agree, sensitively executed and beautifully presented' . . . 'This scheme would be a great asset to the borough' . . . 'Approved unanimously'. The last frame reveals the 'scheme'. It is a giant cheque, made out to the council for the sum of £950,000.

By 1983, alarm bells were sounding over the implementation of

Section 52. A nervous little circular was issued by the DoE offering guidance on planning applications:

The question of imposing a condition or obligation – whether negative or positive in character – should arise only where it is considered that it would not be reasonable to grant a permission in the terms sought which is not subject to such condition or obligation. A wholly unacceptable development should not of course be permitted just because of extraneous benefits offered by the developer.

Applicants had also been complaining that Section 52 agreements had been used by uncooperative councils to delay negotiations over developments, causing expensive delays. The DoE duly wagged a finger. Planning-gain agreements

may well assist towards securing the best use of land and a properly planned environment. But this does not mean that an authority is entitled to treat an applicant's need for permission as an opportunity to obtain some extraneous benefit or advantage or as an opportunity to exact a payment for the benefit of ratepayers at large. Nor should the preparation of such an agreement be permitted to delay unduly the decision on the application.

Section 52, government warnings notwithstanding, is beginning to look well worn and grubby these days. It has been abused both by councils, to stall, and by developers, to blandish. Community architecture offers an alternative bargaining counter. If a developer is able to pull on board an architect who will assemble members of the local community, explain the aims of the scheme and suggest a menu of community benefits that local people can choose from, then that developer has a running start with the council, which has neither the time nor the staff to consult in this way. The architect's role, however, has changed significantly from 'enabler' to locum. The architect acts as stand-in for the local council in consulting the residents, but also as stand-in for the developer in setting the parameters of public intervention.

You get a better run for your money if you promise a 'community' scheme. It is shorthand for, 'This product has been prepared in accordance with the principles of the Prince of Wales and is guaranteed to be free from high-handed professional arrogance. We strongly urge approval by the planning committee, who will see a lot of mileage in the "community" angle.'

The aims of any architect working with a community are clear, because those aims evolve in discussion with the people directly affected by development. The aims of an architect hired by a developer are subject to more diverse pressures, for the architect is not only doing his or her job but also that of the 'philanthropic' developer, together with that of the local authority, whose statutory role it is to represent local people. It is a difficult business, community architecture in advance of a real brief, and with a client who is not the user client. In a way it is less symptomatic of architects colonizing further the market in professional arbitration and more symptomatic of the further withdrawal from the public arena of the public sector itself. Section 52 has always put planners at a disadvantage, because, as planning-gain consultant Richard Fordham says, 'Planners are not generally numerate, while developers are.'

This is how planning gain works in practice. Big Ugly Sheds plc, the DIY megastore chain, wants to build a superstore on a derelict site. No, say the planners, this area is zoned for industrial and office use and what you propose is a non-food retail warehouse. So what? says Big Ugly Sheds. What difference does it make? Nobody's going to build anything else there, and our 'non-food retail warehousing' scheme will create 200 jobs locally. No, say the planners. It is out of scale, it is too big. Fine, says the developer, I'll take it down in size by 10 per cent. No, say the planners. This scheme is bound to generate a lot of traffic; your car-parking provision is inadequate. OK, says the developer, I'll increase car parking by 15 per cent. Well, say the planners, we'll have to talk about community gain. What's that? says the developer. It's what we used to call planning gain before the Prince of Wales taught us that 'community' is an adjective, say the planners. We'll have to negotiate a Section 52 agreement.

The planners go into a huddle with Big Ugly Sheds, which promises to pay for a service-access road and a new sports pavilion a mile away to compensate for the loss of some public open space and a football pitch which is destined to disappear under part of the new Big Ugly Shed. The developer also promises to buy some new play equipment for the park a mile away and pay for its maintenance. On paper, it looks like an impressive deal for the local authority. Road improvements will cost around £200,000, the pavilion and play equipment another £250,000, maintenance is commuted to a lump sum of £40,000 and there will be some new landscaping worth £15,000. The planners add it all up: outline planning consent brings £505,000 in planning gain for the community. It's a deal.

But how much of that money represents true gain? Most of the work the developer is paying for is occasioned by the development itself. There would be no need for a new road if the Big Ugly Shed didn't go there; the provision of a pavilion and play equipment is 'in kind' compensation for the loss of the public open space and football pitch, which is being taken out by development; likewise for the maintenance payment. The total planning gain achieved by our fictitious planners in this little fable comes to £15,000 worth of shrubs and borders.

Councils are finding it hard to fight their corner these days. The pressure for development is intense, and the penalties for opposing (without a demonstrably good reason) a development scheme are heavy: inquiry costs can be awarded against the council. It is suggested that in the near future costs might actually be awarded against recalcitrant councillors themselves. But there is an amorphous electorate out there, and it can alter the pattern of political power.

Genuine popular opposition to a proposed development is a more dreadful spectre than blustering planners, and developers – especially those bidding in competition – are beginning to see the glimmer of new strategies. Public opposition which causes delay can cost, on paper, a fortune; developers are recognizing that it is more cost-effective to consult the local community from the start and establish some good public relations. Planners will increasingly say, 'Who are we to judge what the people want? If you want a Big Ugly Shed there, we'll call a meeting and you can hear what people think of the idea. If they're happy, we're happy.' If the local residents have access to a technical aid centre they might be able to hire in, for zero outlay, a planner or architect to advise them. She or he might suggest that a new pavilion a mile away is not the best deal they can get. She or he might even propose as essential the appointment by Big Ugly Sheds of an architect rather than a shed-maker for the scheme. In the arcane battle of wills that is urban planning today, it is important that the people who live in the neighbourhood have the same access to professional help as the people who want to stake a claim in it. Legal Aid allows access to professional help in the courts; why should there not be a system of Architectural Aid which provides expert guidance for those who have neighbourhoods to defend or improve?

When the Prince of Wales talks about the forces which have shaped, or distorted, the look of our country, the influence of town-planning legislation is conspicuous by its absence. Yet the power of planners is paramount: they administer the rules. Planning is a post-war invention. Sir Edwin Lutyens and his Victorian predecessors did not have to cope with it. Sir Alfred Waterhouse did not have to sit through interminable planning delays. There were no Section 52 negotiations for the ever-resourceful and entrepreneurial John Nash. The current deployment of the 1971 Planning Act must inevitably be traced back to the manipulations of local-planning officers in their efforts to wring benefit from planning deals on behalf of councils who were deprived of other means.

As we enter a new era of neighbourhood politics, it will be up to residents themselves to decide who should represent them in the planning forum: planners who are responsible to officers who are responsible to the people, or architects employed by the people themselves. Architects are ready to act as their attorneys.

11

Community Engineering

The first reference to community architecture I can remember was a television programme about Black Road in Macclesfield. There was an architect, Rod Hackney, scrabbling about in jeans and Dr Marten's with the residents of sixty-odd condemned houses. He had bought one of them in order to finish his PhD after returning from Scandinavia, where he had been working with the Danish architect Arne Jacobsen.

Hackney's considerable skill in motivating people resulted in a residents' campaign to save the houses. They hammered at the local council until the neighbourhood was declared a General Improvement Area. The residents formed a trust and delegated powers to a committee; they made a loud noise which was impossible for the local authority to ignore. After a struggle, the council gave in: the residents, who had bought their homes for next to nothing from a private landlord, won a £130,000 improvement-grant package and secured the future of Black Road both as a place to live and as an icon of self-help, a philosophy which was only just edging into the frame then – the early 1970s – but which was to become the clarion call of Conservatism a decade later. What united the architects from all over the country, working on very different schemes, was a common pattern of practice.

In the 1970s, endless angst-ridden conferences were held and countless papers written on the future of housing in Britain. Several had the same title: Whither the public sector? By the early 1980s, they'd started dropping the 'h'.

The creation of a property-owning democracy was a piecemeal affair. Housing-improvement grants allowed people to pay for repairs to individual homes; a new concept of 'enveloping' allowed grant aid for whole streets to be given a communal facelift. Those distributing the money soon cottoned on to the fact that there was economy in numbers. Why pay out fifty or 100 separate grants when you could get a more cost-effective deal by getting the whole lot done in one go? The idea of enveloping depended on everyone in the street being in on it. It was so much easier if everyone wanted the same thing. This is what architects realized, too. The time had come for small-scale collective action. The climate was right: here was work for underemployed architects. The 1969 Housing Act introduced the concepts of the general improvement area and the housing action area. It was a kind of social dividend – IMF to HMG, HMG to HAA, HAA to you and me. Better realpolitik than no spending on housing at all, and it kept the lump-labour builders off the dole queue.

The early 1970s marked the deepest economic trough of the post-war period in Britain. Architects, like everybody else, felt the pinch. I started my practice in Islington in 1972. By 1973 there were six of us and we were just starting to earn a decent living. By 1974 we were down to two and living courtesy of our bank manager. We, like any architects, were delighted to take on an improvement-grant job or two.

Community architecture's main characteristic, the whole *point* of community architecture, is that it is labour-intensive. Its nature is determined not by architectural skills but by leadership skills, counselling skills. You're not creating architecture but forming a community, and this was what gave the exponents of community architecture such a buzz – this was the architecture not of a built environment but of people. Or rather, it was a kind of community engineering. In run-down streets where there had existed an anthology of individual miseries there was now a collective optimism. People had been galvanized, positively charged with a new will.

In all the accounts of Black Road and other 'pioneering' schemes, the residents say the same thing: that the experience of suddenly being defined as a community turned strangers into neighbours, neighbours into co-workers, colleagues into mates. The architect's role was that of a social development officer, mucking in and taking the brass – if there was any brass. Although the potential assets of private householders stood a good chance of rising sharply with environmental improvements – the market value of a Black Road house went from £500 to £20,000 – there was often little money to fund the schemes and pay professional fees.

A lot of architects, however, had time on their hands. From the three-day week to Michael Heseltine's moratoria, public-sector housing shrivelled to the stump it now is. Working on spec with the promise of a fee when the grant came in offered architects the chance to spend their time, which was cheap, doing something interesting and, in the journalistic parlance of the time, to become street-credible. You could tell the architects from the clients only by the back pocket of their Levi's, which held a rolled-up copy of the *New Musical Express* instead of the *Sun*.

An evolutionary trigger mechanism caused a sort of melanism in young, eager and unemployed architects, who acted like those butterflies that changed their camouflage during the Industrial Revolution to blend in with a built environment that got grubbier and grubbier. Gone was the gentleman-architect, the kind you used to recognize by the cut of his jib and the rakish insouciance of his bow tie. This new generation of 'enablers' sent back the Moss Bros. suit and started to shave less often. They set up Tretchikov half-lives in flats among the residents, on 'twenty-four hour alert'. A take-away curry might at any moment be interrupted by an anxious 'user' in a dilemma over the landscaping. Over endless cups of tea they passed their brief back again and again for further refinement to an initially bewildered group of consumers who didn't know much about art but after a bit of coaxing knew what they didn't like – leaky roofs and vandals. These architects dressed down in undergraduate mufti, the egalitarian uniform of the oppressed. From the winter of discontent through to the inner-city riots a new brood of architects was incubated who shrugged off the user-based message of modernism. The modern movement had to be wrong; it was old. Here were architects who struck a challenging stance, unencumbered by a workload. To describe the process of user-led development, they talked of 'bottom-up' architecture. It had a gratifyingly coarse ring to it, as if the self-styled new wave of practitioners really were the 'punks' of the profession, mooning at the rest of us from a battered Transit van.

Having mobilized community groups and interested the media, the New Age architects looked on their works and were well pleased. Public opinion had come full circle. Architects had once stood in the dock on a trumped-up charge of 'social engineering'. Now suddenly we were being exhorted to do it for real. In the midst of a DIY boom, we were the Mr Fixits. is your community in need of repair? Do you and your neighbours need bathroom extensions and gardens? Nobody to turn to? Don't despair . . .

Money, as ever, was the key factor. Community architects found new ways of unlocking new kinds of financial aid. It had nothing to do with architecture. It was simply a methodology of its time, and people had to work together to make it happen. The ever-adaptable architect found a way of channelling the energies of the 'community' into achievable aims – getting the neighbourhood declared a General Improvement Area, for example. Instead of collecting architectural drawings, residents would collect press cuttings (angry residents up in arms are the staple diet of local newspapers) and lay siege to the local planning offices. Councils would reach first for the aspirins and then for the chequebook.

For a while, community architecture was capital's plaything. Money had quit industry and the welfare state and was amusing itself with minor entertainments. Money discovered community architecture, rescued it from the gutter and glamorized it. And then tired of it. Now capital is back in the major league, backing private-sector renewal. Community architecture, whatever it may be and whatever its supporters claim for it, has been eclipsed in the urban regenerative process by the boom in developer-led schemes. Now community architects are looking for new ways to fit into the jigsaw.

It is interesting to compare two projects by Hunt Thompson, an energetic practice who have done much to raise the profile of community-based schemes. The first is the Lea View House scheme in Hackney, east London.

The local council decided to chance its arm with an imaginative reworking of an old and ghastly five-storey block of flats which was run-down and hard to let. Architects moved into an empty flat and held a succession of meetings with the tenants to discuss improvements. The result was a stunningly imaginative work of recycling and building, opening blank walls to accommodate new entrances with a secure, private-sector feel – the creation of what environmental determinists call 'defensible space'.

The term was coined by the American architect Oscar Newman and gained a great deal of credibility in the 1970s. Its premise was that if you replace large, anonymous 'communal' space with sectioned spaces assigned to individual units, allowing nosey neighbours to keep a check on the comings and goings, it will lead to a decline in antisocial behaviour. Although his thesis has been taken up enthusiastically in this country by academics like Alice Coleman and more 'progressive' elements in the DoE, Newman is largely regarded as something of an historical curiosity in the States. New housing projects offering apartments for sale in New York are marketed as having defended, rather than defensible, space. 'Security guard on permanent patrol' is today's selling point.

The Lea View House project rearranged and modified flats in a five-storey, 300-home estate in Clapton built in 1939. By the time Hunt Thompson were appointed by Hackney Borough Council in 1981, the 660 residents had joined the growing numbers of local-authority tenants marooned in a deteriorating, shrinking public estate. The block's structure was decaying, resident caretakers had been removed, community facilities terminated and the local rent office shut. A project office was opened in one of the empty flats, from where a social survey was carried out. Proposals were approved and work started in April 1982 on phase one of the scheme – eighty units at a project cost of £2.3 million. Phase two, a further 165 units, cost around £4 million. The building contract was placed with the council's own direct-labour organization. Internally, the layout was changed. Maisonettes were formed by combining flats on the ground and first floors; new stairs and lifts separated access for upper-floor flats. Externally, front gardens and a communal landscaped garden were created; doors and gable ends were pedimented; new lift shafts were livened up with jazzy banded brickwork and shallow pyramidal roofs; window frames were painted in bright colours. Post-modern architectural bricollage was added to make the public-sector estate look like a private-sector one. Management systems were changed and communications improved between tenants and the local council, who, along with the architects, share the credit for promoting such a progressive and enlightened scheme. They also put up the money.

The scheme was a triumph, an estate modernization characterized by close consultation with the users, as all good architecture is characterized. From Dead End Street to Sesame Street – this was community architecture mark one. Since the completion of the Lea View House project, its methods and its success have become, for community architects, a legend. Legendary in the real sense: the tale has been told and retold so often that its achievements are seen to reach far beyond the prosaic, though innovative, refurbishment of a council block. 'Men get opinions as boys learn to spell: by reiteration, chiefly,' wrote Elizabeth Barrett Browning in 1856. The amplified triumph of Lea View House is now a benchmark in the development of community architecture. You can bet that at any given moment someone, somewhere is giving a slide show on the success of Lea View House. It is architecture's King Kong.

Community architecture mark two is best defined by a more recent project involving Hunt Thompson: the regeneration of the Bishopsgate goods-yard site, on the City fringe.

Here, the architects were brought in by one of four developers pitching for the chance to convert ten acres of London's run-down East End into a lucrative office development. The owners were British Rail, whose primary concern was to get the best possible deal from a development partner. But Tower Hamlets Environmental Trust saw the opportunity for 'community involvement' and wrote to all four developers, suggesting they organized a planning exercise with members of the local community. Three of the developers ignored the request, but London and Edinburgh Trust – the developers for the neighbouring Spitalfields Market site – agreed, and called in Hunt Thompson. In great haste, something called a Community Planning Weekend was convened, at which architects, developers and members of the local community could thrash out some basic principles for the scheme and ensure that, as well as the usual mix of high-return offices and flats, the proposals would include something of benefit to the people who already lived and worked there: community gain. But the very short lead-in time to the weekend gave the participants little chance to prepare plans, which had to conform to a draft development brief from joint planning authorities Tower Hamlets and Hackney Borough Councils.

The developers chose wisely in getting Hunt Thompson on the team. The practice is not only one of the best exponents of community engineering; it is also, after Rod Hackney's practice, the most famous. While the developers insisted the community exercise was a genuine attempt to combine commercial viability and social responsibility, more cynical observers suggested it was little more than a publicity stunt. The hiring-in of community architects by the developers rather than local residents alerted Kay Jordan, of the RIBA's own Community Architecture Group, to what she saw as 'bulldozering techniques and complete disregard for any form of collective community approach'. But John Thompson, a senior partner in the practice, defended the architects' involvement. A planning weekend with locals might be good for London and Edinburgh Trust's image, it might improve their chances of getting the site, but the exercise would establish new ground rules for development, he said.

Robert Cowan of the *Architects' Journal* reported a pitifully low turnout for the series of public planning meetings, at which participants moved pieces of card around on a 1:500 map of the site.

Several thousand leaflets were distributed to people living near the goods-yard site inviting them to take part. But only about 10 members of the public came to the Planning for Real session in December, and eight and nine respectively in the two sessions on 24 and 25 January – in the week before the Community Planning Weekend.

Without a model, the participants needed a good deal of guidance as to which part of the site they were considering at any particular moment, and to what the constraints on development were. They were told by the staff of Planning Aid for London, who ran the sessions, that the developer wanted the western end of the site for offices, and that this community planning exercise was a case of 'you scratch my back and I'll scratch yours'. Accordingly all three sessions allocated the western end to offices.

Another part of the site, they were told, was registered in the name of the housing co-op next door – 'and they wouldn't appreciate any use other than housing there'. With full verbal explanations necessary to compensate for the lack of a model, it was possible for participants to make sensible and relevant choices even without quite knowing which part of the base plan related to which part of the site or surrounding area. Even after two hours some participants were not sure which end of the plan represented where they lived.'

London and Edinburgh Trust won the pitch. Their strategy was vindicated. For the architects, it was equally rewarding. Having been drafted in as consultants, they took over as master planners for the site from the original architects. The 'community' is indeed a force to be reckoned with.

Ironically, the Prince of Wales himself has recently criticized the appropriation of 'community architecture' by developers seeking a front. Yet, at Poundbury Farm, the Dorchester overspill town proposed for Duchy of Cornwall land, His Royal Highness is effectively the developer. He had promised full public consultation on plans for the 400-acre site, which is to be the '10 Commandments' made concrete. Or, rather, made in traditional materials.

The planning weekend held to launch the scheme was, by all accounts, an interesting experience. It illustrates the current difficulty in deciding when public opinion should be wheeled in. A masterplan for the model community has been worked up by urban theorist Leon Krier; indeed, a model of it was on display as part of the consultation process. Its inspiration is classical and its size, as the Prince stressed, is that of medieval Siena.

There has been a large measure of support for the Poundbury scheme from the local authority. Planning approval has been inferred in advance, its popularity underwritten by its sponsor. For the planning weekend, Hunt Thompson were appointed community relations consultants.

Developers have not been slow to recognize the cachet which attaches to schemes claiming to have a community-based philosophy. They have discovered it is possible to transform public opinion about a possibly lucrative scheme by shelling out for a community-architecture element. To hire in a socially responsible architect for an outline scheme costs less than a decent company car. Community architecture is the new planning gain.

12

Breaking the Code

Architects changed their job description before the Prince of Wales changed his. It is no coincidence that the emergence of architects using the 'revolutionary' methods of community architecture was at a time of fundamental change in the way practice and professional behaviour were controlled by the Royal Institute of British Architects.

Ancient restrictions in the Institute's Code of Professional Conduct and bye-laws were swept away in a major reform. The early 1980s saw the end of mandatory fee scales, the end of a professional ban on architects operating as developers and company directors and the end of severe restrictions on the way architects were allowed to market and advertise their services.

Market forces, government intervention through the Monopolies Commission and the growth of a related PR industry combined to legitimize new patterns of practice. One of the first practices to demonstrate how architects might create new opportunities from these changed circumstances was Rock Townsend, an enterprising practice headed by David Rock and John Townsend which had attracted much praise for their community workspaces at Barley Mow and Dryden Street in Covent Garden – imaginative internal reworkings of old industrial buildings to form largely open-plan office accommodation with shared services and management. Rock was among the first to articulate the kinds of possibilities open to architects because of changes to the Code. A growing number of people were becoming aware of the new horizons open to them by becoming architect/developers and controlling more closely all aspects of project development.

I supported the Code changes completely. I once wrote a paper in which I argued that if it was legitimate to advertise contraceptives, it ought to be legitimate to advertise architecture. There had been uproar in the RIBA in the late 1970s when the first tentative proposals to scrap the restrictions surfaced to entrenched opposition from the traditionalists. There was a moral argument which said the profession should not be encumbered by restrictive rules framed by long-dead aristocrats from a lost world of privilege and snobbery. There was also a strong commercial argument. How could the architect, already facing a downturn in the amount of work coming in, hope to compete in the brash new marketplace of Thatcherite Britain? We were bound and gagged.

Those of us who argued for change rejected the charge that if our rules went out of the window, so would our principles. People became architects to serve their art and the people it sheltered; petty and archaic rules simply got in the way. As the clamour for and against change grew within the RIBA, its president, Gordon Graham, formed the Code Policy Committee to focus the arguments. I was one of its members. Others included Jack Whittle (former Cheshire county architect), David Waterhouse (grandson of the celebrated Victorian architect) and Maurice McCarthy (an architect with the London Borough of Hillingdon who has made almost a second career for himself by campaigning against alleged constitutional improprieties within the Institute). All men. There were two administrative assistants drafted in: Joyce Lynch and Inga Taylor. Both women. This, as it turned out, was to be highly significant.

The committee members were there to weigh carefully the issues raised by deregulation; to apply, as David Waterhouse insisted, deontology – the science of ethics. It was one of the most challenging times I have ever experienced within the Institute. It was genuine intellectual work: was this or that right or wrong? At the time you weren't allowed to have your name more than 2 inches high on a brass plate outside your door. I and others wondered what was really wrong with having your name 2 feet high if you wanted. A walk down any main road would show you that everyone else had. And the Trades Descriptions Act was there to protect the consumer from false claims and control the way in which we all operated. Anyway, it all seemed so silly. Having your name more than 2 inches high on a brass plate was made to seem like not wearing a tie in the dining room. It simply wasn't *done*.

We might have agonized for ever, had it not been for Joyce Lynch and Inga Taylor, who turned their support role into the driving force of the committee. They saw this as a major opportunity to change the world of architecture and make a large dent in the pomposity of architects, who were, and regrettably still are, predominantly men. They made no attempt to hide their contempt for the way the RIBA clung to old men's ideals. We used to meet three or four times a month, going through every bye-law and Code clause inside out, and they would drive us forward. Every time we seemed to weaken, to relent and suggest that we retain this or that control, they would say, 'This is nothing to do with architecture. This isn't ethics. This is a club rule.' From time to time, the anxious faces of senior RIBA officials would appear round the door, wide-eyed, saying, 'You can't do this. You can't let people advertise / become directors of property companies / own manufacturing companies. This isn't a club rule. This is architecture.'

The forces of reaction tried to stop it. The establishment wanted as much distance between the architect and the general public as possible, but they were now living in a changed world. There lingered a small but disproportionately influential coterie of nostalgics who saw the Institute exclusively as a learned society. While the very fabric of our towns and cities was falling apart, here were people talking about classicism and tradition. They shared the Prince of Wales's vision of Britain but lacked his social interest. They preferred Architecture to architecture, feeling instinctively that working with council tenants on a community refurbishment scheme was dragging the profession downmarket. What those of us who broke the Code were up against was resistance on a grand scale.

The economic realities were that public building, and new building generally, was down. Refurbishment was up. Everywhere, local authorities were having to make do and mend. Practices like mine, which started up in the 1970s, were taking any work they could get and were grateful for it. And we were good at it. We lavished as much care and energy on an estate refurb as we would have done on a country home. It was a job we had trained for seven years to do. Our public image, though, was not helping us to get work. The signal beamed out by the traditionalists was that architects were artists, not artisans. Meanwhile, a growing proportion of a dwindling number of refurbishment schemes were being managed by building surveyors, who had started to market their profession in an aggressive and successful way.

Ever since some of architecture's leading lights had too readily accepted the blame for Ronan Point and a housing stock left to rot, we had all laboured under a professional crisis of confidence. But ordinary architects were becoming increasingly frustrated, and increasingly resentful of the inherited guilt about post-war housing they were expected to carry. The commandments of the RIBA no longer struck terror into the hearts of the new pragmatists. If they had a chance to work on a well-conceived but under-funded inner-city scheme for less than the mandatory fee, they would. If the RIBA threatened them with expulsion, it would be the RIBA's loss. To some architects, subscriptions were looking like luxuries they could ill afford.

One of those architects to whom the rules and regulations were totally irrelevant was Rod Hackney. He had seen the future: it was less time at the drawing board, more time with the users, running a property and development company, ad hoc financial deals and good PR. He broke the rules and didn't care. He and others displayed a nonchalant attitude to comments about code contraventions. The gentlemen players were outraged. At the behest of the Government, the Monopolies and Mergers Commission was looking very sternly indeed at the mandatory fee scale for architects. Everybody was supposed to be closing ranks; yet here were architects brazenly challenging the status quo and – worse still – working cheap.

Pressure from within and reforms imposed by the Commission combined in 1981 to liberate the profession from the old restrictions. Suddenly, it was all gone. Architects were free to advertise their services and able to practice in a new *laissez-faire* spirit. The stage was set for a change of image for architects. On the day it became legal, I placed an ad in *The Times*. We were free to market specialist skills not just in restaurants to potential clients to whom we had been recommended by a friend of a friend, but on the streets to people who, along with their neighbours, needed a new bathroom extension and wanted help getting a grant. Architects had built a new stage; all they needed was an audience.

13
Nouveaux Pauvres

The marketing infrastructure was in place, but what were architects selling? Nobody bought architecture, they just paid for it. What architects sold was themselves. Instead of skills, architects sold services. 'Clients' became 'customers' or 'users'; 'commissions' became 'jobs'. And if there were only ordinary jobs for them to do, they would *make* them special. If they didn't have the opportunity to find new ways of building, they would find new ways of practising.

Whether you were having an exploratory talk with a residents' association who wanted a new community hall or starting a refurb scheme at a block of council flats, the idea of discussing the 'brief' with the 'client' had to be redefined. You were working for no-budget community groups or local authorities who had neither the time nor the staff to carry out social surveys or assign an on-site liaison officer. Community architects were happy to step into the gap and pleased to be working with the users. There wasn't any money at all on schemes that needed a feasibility study carried out first. The architect's mission was to work, for nothing, on a plan of action to attract some grant aid. So the architects spent the things that really mattered – time and energy.

Community architects, like their commercial counterparts, were free to bargain. Fees were negotiable, deals could be made. While there was a commercial drift towards one-stop architecture, into project management and design and build, in which the client is offered an integrated package of services from planning application to carpet tiles, community architects offered a more self-effacing role. This has now been eclipsed by proprietorial wrangling over community architecture's provenance. The message from both ends of the profession, however, was the same – that what the client was buying was a *process*.

It was an economic climate, rather than community architecture, which changed public perception of what architects are good at. In the old days, an architect was someone hired in by corporate means. A local authority or a company would commission an architect. Private commissions were regarded as a self-indulgence; architects called in by the *nouveaux riches* to design a swanky apartment or country retreat. This was always a distorted view but one reinforced by the world of architectural criticism, which lavished much attention on the glossier aspects of design and largely ignored the more prosaic accounts of architects working with ordinary people on ordinary schemes. Private clients with a few bob to spend on a new home or a tasteful stables conversion would contact the RIBA and initiate a search through the Institute's Clients Advisory Service. This acts as a matchmaker: it keeps on file details of practices and their portfolios and supplies prospective clients with a short list of likely practices. Architects are given a form to fill in, with little boxes to tick to indicate the kind of work done in the past. The temptation is to be panicked into lying about your portfolio, to tick the maximum number of boxes and increase your chances of a commission. 'Have you done an abattoir?' 'Well, no, I haven't done an abattoir but I did have a Big Mac once . . .' Tick. 'Have you done a dental surgery?' 'Well, no, but I once had a tooth crowned . . .' Tick. There was a feeling that you wouldn't get to do an abattoir unless you'd already done one. The emphasis in the 1980s, however, is on the *way* you practise, the process itself, and the chances are that if you're good at abattoirs, you're good at dental surgeries.

The newly liberated architects who saw themselves as enablers, though, found little resonance in the market for posh houses. They were putting their energies into street-level architecture; the predilections of the *nouveaux riches* were marginal and meaningless. For the ragged-trousered philanthropists of the architectural profession, salvation lay in the creation of a new economic class: the *nouveaux pauvres*.

The wave of new legislation on housing which swept the country from 1979 to 1984 underlined the Government's determination to create a property-owning democracy in which the majority would continue to vote Tory. The Housing Act and the right-to-buy legislation focused attention as never before on the sleeping giant of home equity. It was all very well for the Prince of Wales to tell us that community architecture was the way forward, but the ends presupposed the means. The pressure for home ownership is a major factor in the rapid expansion of two demographic groups: the home-owner and the homeless. The number of private householders was around 7 million in the early 1960s; by the end of the 1970s it stood at around 10 million; by 1987 the figure was 14.5 million and rising. In a parallel pitch on the graph, homelessness rose by 44,000 between 1981 and 1987, to 118,000. The economic effect was to create a new intermediate class, a social phenomenon which crystallized around the premise of rising property values. The rich man in his castle, the poor man at his gate, and suddenly we were all sorcerer's apprentices in Mama Doc's voodoo republic. The spell only worked, however, if you had a mortgage.

The rich, like the poor, are always with us. There have always been two kinds of rich: the eternal rich, who have ancestry and the dumb reasoning of class economics behind them, and the *nouveaux riches*, who have money acquired in the current generation. The parvenus of the 1980s who have largely dictated fashion and style came to be known as yuppies. The word passed swiftly from a cabal of smart New Yorkers into common usage. Everybody knows what it means and nobody, of course, is one.

There are now two kinds of poor. There are the poor who are always with us, who have nothing. These are the people even Lord Scarman and other peers cannot reach. Now, though, there are the *nouveaux pauvres*, people who have nothing but their homes. Just as the 1980s have seen us learning to call money credit, so 'home' has been redefined as 'equity'. In the mad summer of 1988, when estate agents became croupiers at the gaming tables of popular capitalism, the talk in wine bars, pubs, restaurants, living rooms and offices was of little else. The old axiom of a roof over your head was only as valid as the last surveyor's report. The *nouveaux pauvres* had limited income but a substantial realizable asset, and it was rising.

Community architects had their most conspicuous successes with property in private ownership. Houses which might have been bulldozed in a national housing plan were saved, bought and improved by people, under the expert guidance of architects. In the early days, when there was little prospect of making any money out of it, architects would defy the old mandatory fee scales and work for next to nothing. The experience was rewarding in itself. If an on-spec feasibility study led to a financed project, the architect would get a fee. If not, too bad. Having recognized that the things worth spending are time and money, community architects generally went along with the Government's doctrinaire Third World line on inner-city deprivation: that you can't solve a problem by 'throwing money at it'. There was a caveat that if the problem was poverty, throwing money at it wasn't a bad idea, but it took a while for this notion to catch on.

14

New and Secondhand

In 1984, at Hampton Court, the Prince of Wales came to dinner. Too late, his hosts – the RIBA – realized they were the main course.

The Prince had accepted an invitation to be guest of honour at the event, the culmination of celebrations to mark the 150th anniversary of the RIBA, and to present the annual Royal Gold Medal to architect Charles Correa. His speech, had it been delivered by anyone else, would have been ignored, but in the space of a few minutes, the heir to the throne helped wreck two major schemes for London, at Mansion House Square and the National Gallery, and put a curse on the profession as a whole. Architects, he said, had 'consistently ignored the feelings and wishes of the mass of ordinary people in this country'.

Part of the profession was exempted from the ticking off. Those who described themselves as 'community architects' were immune rom the dreaded Lurgi. The effect of the Prince of Wales's intervention on the subject of community architecture was to divide the architectural profession, suddenly and arbitrarily, into goodies and baddies.

'To be concerned about the way people live, about the environment they inhabit and the kind of community that is created by that environment, should surely be one of the prime requirements of a really good architect. It has been most encouraging to see the development of community architecture as a natural reaction to the policy of decamping people to new towns and overspill estates, where the extended family patterns of support were destroyed and community life was lost. Now, moreover, we are seeing the gradual expansion of housing co-operatives, particularly in the inner-city areas of Liverpool, where the tenants are able to work with an architect of their own who listens to their comments and their ideas and tries to design the kind of environment they want, rather than the kind which tends to be imposed upon them without any degree of choice.'

The reference to Liverpool was inspired by the work of the Eldonians, a housing co-operative which fought both the Conservative Government and the Militant-controlled local authority to rebuild their neighbourhood after the closure of the Tate and Lyle factory, the major local employer. The community and their architects presented a swashbuckling example of self-help and determination in their struggle to secure the future of a Roman Catholic neighbourhood. Their efforts are universally admired by architects; but the implication made by the Prince of Wales was that as this was an example of community architecture, those architects who did not declare themselves to be part of the crusade must necessarily be on the wrong side of the front line.

Later in the speech he drew comfort from the fact that there was 'a growing number of architects prepared to listen and to offer imaginative ideas'. The idea was firmly planted in the public imagination that the majority of architects, therefore, were not. For those who chose to characterize themselves as freedom fighters trying to change the architectural profession from within, the Prince's support was elevated to the status of a rallying cry. It no longer mattered that the alleged 'enemies' of community architecture did not exist. With the Prince of Wales as a friend, who needed enemies? Architecture had largely been a closed book to the media. Now the subject was enlivened by a crusading Prince and a snappy phrase which was easy to understand. If this was the acceptable face of architecture, reasoned the journalists, the rest was clearly unacceptable. Architects went back to their practices the morning after the speech with the newspapers pointing the finger at a new face in the line-up of tabloid monsters. Murderers, hooligans, unstable foreign heads of state and the National Union of Mineworkers were now joined by the culpable architect, who certainly had a lot to answer for. The *Mojahadeen* of community architecture did not merely acquiesce as the conviction deepened; they sought actively to promote the idea. Community architecture became a shibboleth for the profession. You were either with it or against it.

The nebulous characteristics of community architecture were both a puzzle to and a blessing for ordinary practices. As far as we could gather, the basic principle was that you consulted the users and involved them as far as possible in the design process. That was *it*? Perfect. In meetings held by practices up and down the country the morning after the speech, there was just one item on the agenda. As the Alka Seltzer fizzed, architectural minds untrained in the arts of PR posed the question: 'What are the implications of this in terms of marketing our practice?' For 'community' was the new wonder ingredient and it suddenly became the prefix everybody wanted. Firms looked at what they had on their books, everything from the rehabilitation of crumbling council blocks to consultation work with English Heritage, and said, 'This is already community architecture. We've been community architects all along. Put it in the brochure.' They didn't have to change a thing; they just had to rename it. It soon got out of hand: 'We do quinquennial surveys of an eighteenth-century church. That's community architecture. We did a scheme for the local GP. That's community architecture.'

This was, ultimately, the supreme triumph of community architecture. It was a PR coup on a massive scale. The newly emboldened chosen few started taking themselves very seriously indeed. They were suddenly symbolic of a 'quiet revolution' and they were damned if they weren't going to shout their heads off about it. Support from the Prince, a supreme representative of an establishment which both owned the City yet was apparently powerless to stop its destruction, put the fire of publicity in their bellies. They were on a mission. It wasn't, however, an architectural uprising; this was no battle of the styles. They wanted to renounce publicly their mystery and craft, to say to ordinary people, 'We're one of you, just like the Prince of Wales.' They evangelized with a religious fervour, daring others to challenge the unchallengeable. For what were you saying if you opposed community architecture? That you *didn't* believe in user-led design? That people *aren't* important? That they *don't* deserve an environment they have helped to create?

Community architects turned professional elitism on its head. Having rejected what they saw as the traditional approach, they set up an alternative, and largely intuitive, 'code of practice' defined less by what it was than by what it wasn't. The architect should not be remote from the building user, should not impose his or her will in a 'top-down' approach. This was common sense in the late 1970s and early 1980s, with few opportunities for the kind of imperious environmental ego-tripping community architects so rightly despised. We operate in a changeable economic climate in which construction activity is inextricably linked to available finance. Much of the profession's workload was small scale at the time. An increasingly consumerist society expected, demanded, choice. Architects simply could not ignore the preferences of building users. Architects were being commissioned more and more as consultants, and what should a consultant do if not consult? In terms of architectural practice, form followed function. Talking to people about the kind of environment they wanted was the difference between good and bad architecture. Community architects made a virtue of necessity.

In the 1960s, architects were working on large housing projects and were separated from the end users. The designers of new public housing were nearly always designing for hypothetical clients with hypothetical needs. In the 1970s, architects were in touch with users much more as a matter of course; with new-build budgets slashed, refurbishment work formed a much greater part of architects' workload. Like many others my practice did its best to persuade councils out of the habit of 'decanting' tenants during improvement work. It was a tremendously disruptive process and further alienated the tenants from the architecture itself. Even the word 'decant' has a horribly insensitive connotation in the context of social housing. It says you are chucking people out of their homes while you improve and redecorate to your standards and taste. We published a booklet called *Tenanted Refurbishment: The Community Way* in 1984. It outlined an established method of social housing improvement that had seemed plain common sense to many architects and which I suppose would these days be called 'community architecture'. For years we had simply regarded it as good practice. If a local authority wanted to commission a refurbishment scheme from us, the following guidelines would have to be followed:

1. The architectural team moves in and makes a survey of physical conditions, tenants' worries, environmental patterns.

2. Analysis of survey followed by development of proposals possible within budget for presentation to local authority.

3. Public discussion with all tenants about proposals, followed by vote about the overall scheme and its details.

4. Redesign approved by local authority and tenants and start on production drawings as basis for tenders.

5. Tenders called from selected list of contractors and contract let.

6. Permanent on-site architect appointed for duration of the contract acting as supervisor and informal on-site complaints bureau.

7. Contractor clears council's backlog of defects and maintenance before starting work.

8. Preliminary meeting with tenant, architect and builder's representative before work starts on each flat.

9. Regular monthly surgeries/tenant meetings set up.

10. Just before practical completion of job final tenant debriefing meeting called to ensure that all the work has been done, to get feedback on the running of the job and to explain how handover back to local authority departments will proceed.

To be honest, this approach benefited not only the tenant but also the architect. It was immeasurably more satisfying to work closely with the people whose homes you were improving, getting to know them and winning their trust. The on-site job architect would, when the building work was almost complete, bring the wallpaper catalogues and paint charts, details of floor finishes, bathroom suites and kitchen units. If the architect and tenants were adamant, the local authority and the contractor could be bullied into changing the specification to allow maximum individual choice. There was no mystique involved in working successfully with a community. You listened hard and stayed on call. It was the difference between a good architect and a bad one.

However, the definition of community architecture was always, for its practitioners, difficult. It was easier to revive a collective guilt over shoddy building in the 1960s and invent a contemporary architectural profession which sought to continue to perpetrate the sins of the past. In a checklist published in 1987, written by Nick Wates and Charles Knevitt and subtitled *What Makes Community Architecture Different*, the characteristics of conventional architecture and community architecture are compared.

The 'expert's role' in both was enunciated. The conventional architect was a 'provider, neutral bureaucrat, elitist, "one of them", manipulator of people to fit the system, a professional in the institutional sense. Remote and inaccessible'. The community architect was an 'enabler, facilitator and social entrepreneur, educator, "one of us", manipulator of the system to fit the people and challenger of the status quo, a professional as a competent and efficient adviser, locally based and accessible'.

The conventional 'method of operation' was 'Top-down, emphasis on product rather than process, bureaucratic, centralised with specialisms compartmentalised, stop-go, impersonal, anonymous, paper management, avoid setting a precedent, secretive'. The community method was 'Bottom-up, emphasis on process rather than product, flexible, localised, holistic and multi-disciplinary, evolutionary, continuous, personal, familiar, people management, setting precedents, open'.

The conventional architect was 'Self-conscious about style; most likely "international" or "modern movement". Increasingly one of the other fashionable styles; post-modern, high-tech, neo-vernacular or classical revival. Restrained and sometimes frigid; utilitarian'. Community architects were 'unself-conscious about style. Any style may be adopted as appropriate. Most likely to be contextual, regional (place-specific) with concern for identity. Loose and sometimes exuberant; often highly decorative, using local artists'.

Apostles of doctrinaire community architecture stopped short of comparing, say, 'dress sense'. If they had, the definitions might have run: 'Black hats' and 'White hats'. Everybody makes the arbitrary division of architecture into good or bad, depending on taste. Many people love Quinlan Terry's riverside scheme at Richmond. I dislike it intensely. Many people, including the Prince of Wales, loathe the National Theatre. I love it. The most brilliant examples of community architecture wore their styles as modestly or brazenly as any other architectural scheme. Was Black Road in Macclesfield, the seminal self-help scheme masterminded by Rod Hackney, not 'utilitarian' and 'vernacular'? Was Lea View House, Hunt Thompson's copybook refurbishment of a council block, not fashionable, 'post-modern' even, in its stylish use of pedimented porches and campanile-like lift shafts?

The fact is that community architecture's credo remained in the first person singular: it was whatever you wanted it to be, as long as it deployed the architect as enabler. But if, as a practising community architect, you rejected the rules of conventional architecture, why call yourself an architect at all? The theory was that you would, by example, show the rest of the profession the error of its ways and change the very basis of architecture. In practice, the success of the community architecture movement after May 1984 was attributable almost entirely to the Prince's public endorsement. Community architecture in the early days had been an almost degrading way to work. Now, overnight, it was glamorous.

White hats were big box office, a spaghetti Western. The strangers had ridden into Dead End Gulch to find bandits shooting up the place. Intending to pass through, they were implored by the frightened townfolk to stay and protect them. A community architect's gotta do what a community architect's gotta do. They went to see the sheriff, who, powerless to stop the ravages of the desperadoes, had barricaded himself in the jailhouse. He issued them with ammunition and badges – they were all deputies now. White hats, badges, ammunition. Resistance was brief. Dead End Gulch started slowly to return to peace and prosperity. With just a fistful of dollars to show for it, the White Hats mounted up and rode off into the sunset, headed for Tombstone City, where the tumbleweed blew and the streets had been left for dead. Sure, they could clean up the town. But for a few dollars more.

Despite the diversity of community architecture projects, the variations, for the architects themselves, were on a familiar theme. They worked cheap, and for long hours. The feeling grew that if user-led design meant higher levels of commitment, it should also eventually attract higher levels of remuneration. A campaign was started by architects to have community architecture recognized as a sort of subspecies of mainstream architecture, which involved its own particular set of consultancy skills and which should be tied to a special scale of fees which acknowledged this. At first, this was seen by others within the profession as seeking further to divide us. There were many architects who by now were sick and tired of being accused of some kind of ethical deficiency in choosing not to wear the 'I Love Community Architecture' badge. But the bid for higher remuneration also further alienated those perfectly sincere architects who had been working with the community for some time and had put a cross in the box which said 'no publicity'.

As the academic debates rolled on and the internecine squabbling continued – perpetuated in part, it must be said, by the omnipresent figurehead of the Prince himself – valuable work was being carried out, unseen, throughout the land. Responding to the more positive message that professionals from all disciplines in the construction industry should work more closely together, technical aid centres were established in urban areas all over the country. The idea was that architects, landscape architects, surveyors, engineers, planners – as many building consultants as possible – would set up shop together and work on bread-and-butter schemes for community groups. Pioneers of this kind of practice, like Hull architecture school head Tom Woolley, had been operating an urban attorney service like this years before the squabbles started over who invented the term 'community architecture'.

While community architecture was isolating architects from each other, technical aid centres were integrating the experts. The schemes they enabled were in the main unphotogenic and modest – a community centre conversion, a youth club refurb. Technical aid is the real challenge to conventional architecture, because it writes out any hierarchy. The architect is no longer the 'captain of the building team' but simply a member of it. Technical skills were on tap for community groups in much the same way as advice was being offered to individuals at the Citizens' Advice Bureaux. If the help needed was basically surveying, then a surveyor would be put on the case. Engineers and surveyors would likewise be drafted in to work with the group on feasibility studies and all the necessary paperwork to get grant aid.

Consultants working for these centres are expected to check their egos at the front door; the work ethic is strictly egalitarian. This jarred with the 'community architecture movement' within the profession, which saw the architect as prime mover. Their battle for fair pay was all to do with securing fees for architects, who would lead the project. Technical aiders resented the professional imperialism of architects, which, they claimed, clouded the clear objective of cheap practical help for those who could not afford market rates. The insistence of architects on controlling projects also, they claimed, negated the aim of promoting community self-help. Technical aid was the real enabling force, because it simply cleared a way through the jungle of red tape as scout rather than as team leader. While community architects made friendly overtures to technical aiders, telling them they were all on the same side, the technical aid centre architects remained wary and maintained an ideological independence. A further intervention by the Prince of Wales was to widen the gap.

15

Who Killed Community Architecture?

Community architecture was hard to pin down but easy to praise, and the Prince's public support had bestowed glamour on those who bore witness.

With their travelling slide shows and power lunches at Kensington Palace, community architects now had a reputation to keep up. During 1985–6 the RIBA's Community Architecture Group, under the chairmanship of Manchester architect Ian Finlay, held a series of meetings with workers from the voluntary sector, charities and the technical aid movement. The aim was to exorcize the mistrust felt by many outside the architectural profession as a result of community architecture's high profile. How could architects reconcile their professional self-interest in managing community schemes with the demands of those representing the community groups themselves, whose primary objective was to secure professional help cheaply, or for free? After much delicate negotiation, the National Community Partnership was formed, with a common aim of raising public interest in community-led schemes and fighting for adequate funding for user-led projects throughout the country.

A plan was devised by the NCP to launch a National Community Aid Fund, which would raise and channel funds for groups to employ professional help in getting projects off the ground. They were persuaded, however, to delay the launch until November 1986, when the Prince was to give a keynote address at 'Building Communities', a two-day conference on community architecture, planning and design.

The conference was, significantly, not held at the RIBA headquarters in Portland Place. By now the issue of the Prince and the architectural profession had become a political one. RIBA Council had fielded Raymond Andrews as its candidate for the 1987–9 presidency. He had been the masterplanner of the Institute's 150th anniversary festival year – 1984 – which had been shot through the heart by the Prince of Wales's speech at Hampton Court. Rod Hackney's supporters had joined forces with the 'Stuff the RIBA Jubilee' crowd and the royal followers and were supporting Hackney as a rival candidate on a community architecture ticket. The campaigning had been hard and the contest was exciting considerable interest within the profession and at Kensington Palace. It was establishment versus the challenge; festival and carnival.

Less than a week after the 'Building Communities' conference – guest speaker, HRH the Prince of Wales – Hackney was elected president of the RIBA.

The launch of the National Community Aid Fund at the conference was completely overshadowed by the announcement of yet another new inner-city initiative, the Inner City Trust, whose patron was to be the Prince of Wales. This was to raise £10 million for community projects in its first year. A fund-raising campaign inspired by the Band Aid rock concerts – which, incidentally, certainly did no harm to the careers of those who took part – was announced. Inner City Aid moved the National Community Aid Fund into the back seat, with a promise that it would see it all right when the money came in.

It didn't. The pulling power for Inner City Aid was clearly the Prince of Wales himself. It seemed logical that the scale of response to the appeal would be determined by the level of commitment demonstrated by its patron. The Prince left the stage of the Astoria Theatre, London (a downmarket dance hall booked for two days by organizers who obviously recognized the part song and dance had to play in all this) to thunderous applause. It was the high point of the conference, which in the main had been characterized by the insecurity, rather than the confidence, of community architects. They had grimly applauded a succession of tenants, community workers and residents as they one after the other laid into the professional arrogance of architects, and the professions generally. It was a two-day wallow in a warm bath of masochism.

The event had been boycotted by some community groups and picketed by others, because the lead sponsor was property developer Regalian. The company had been buying up council estates and successfully demonstrating that all a lot of municipal housing really needed was money spent on it. It was widely reported – and never definitively refuted – that members of the Battersea Redevelopment Action Group had claimed that Wandsworth Council had evicted more than 500 families 'under false pretences' to sell council houses to Regalian, who had then improved them and sold them on the open market for between £60,000 and £100,000. Shelter had refused to take part. Other absent community groups dismissed the conference as a publicity stunt for community architects.

The success of the conference had everything to do with the Prince of Wales. His presence put, as they say, the royal seal of approval on community architecture. It was no longer a bandwagon but a golden coach. The trouble was that as the Prince's absolutely genuine and proper concern for the inner cities developed, there were more and more golden coaches and a finite number of horses to pull them. According to royal biographer, Anthony Holden, in *Charles, a Biography*, the 'rapid breakthrough in public recognition of community architecture [was] almost entirely due to the prince's promotion of the movement and its ideals'. Yet at the conference which would launch Inner City Aid, 'Charles could not resist the chance for yet another swipe at the modern stylists of the architectural profession. Now the audience grew noticeably restrained, for he was again confusing method with taste as he went on: "I think it is time to resurrect the principles by which classical Greece operated." '

Holden goes on:

Only eight hours later, at a Mansion House dinner, Charles also launched the Prince's Youth Business Trust, which he described as a 'scheme for job-makers rather than job-seekers' . . . Even he should have foreseen the damage that would be done by launching Inner City Aid and the Prince's Youth Business Trust on the same day. By February, less than three months after that heady reception at the Astoria, it had become clear that they could not co-exist.

Inner City Aid had been killed by kindness, it seemed. Only

£33,000 had been raised. It ceased fund-raising in favour of the flourishing Prince's Youth Business Trust, which had a bewildering array of existing charities all clamouring for funds from the same institutions. Inner City Aid director Charles Knevitt resigned. The golden coach was going nowhere.

The failure of Inner City Aid was a blow for the National Community Aid Fund, whose own public appeal for support had been drowned in the razzmatazz surrounding Inner City Aid. It was also a blow for the community architects themselves, whose ideological *jihad* within the profession now modulated into more practical ways of changing architects' attitudes.

The grey area at the heart of the debate had always been the question, 'What is community architecture?' Its supporters often sheepishly disclaimed the title, sensing that in five short years it had degraded through slogan to cliché to metaphor. By 1989, everybody had tacitly accepted that definitions were valueless, that the key to a common aim lay in a common set of practical services offered to community clients. These would be presented in an easily understood list of consultant services (see Appendix) for which, in theory, the architect would charge on an hourly basis. It dispels for ever the romance of community architecture and enshrines the code of good practice which all architects must honour when working for the community. It is anti-glamorous.

Community architecture is dead. It was not simply killed; it was overkilled. It was a PR exercise masquerading as a crusade, and what died was the idea that it was new. If community architecture had not existed, it would have been necessary to invent it. But it did exist, as it always has. The 1980s offered more opportunities for working with community groups, and architects have seized these opportunities with enthusiasm.

The ideals of community architecture are eternal and unimpeachable. Those who choose to call themselves community architects have no enemy in me. It remains for some an instantly readable logo. For those who sought to enter the architectural debate of recent years, it was a designer label, flaunted in public. The originals are still there – working in the RIBA's Community Architecture Group and its Resource Centre at 66 Portland Place. The pale imitations, the camp followers, have moved on. It is time to regroup as an *architectural* community and time to drop the elitist notion that some of us are touched by a special gift. Community architecture is dead; long live architecture.

16

Sheltered Housing for All

London, 1989. The seventeenth floor of a high-rise block. Inside their council flat, a middle-aged couple lock themselves in for the night.

The local authority owns and runs the tower block in which they live, but after dark the corridors and stairways are controlled by brutal and violent teenagers who revel in an unchallenged reign of terror. They are the jailers; they set the curfew.

Victor and Audrey Johnson are terrified of them, like most of the tenants here. But although they are neighbours, the residents are isolated, rather than united, by their common anxieties. People venture out as little as possible. They barricade themselves against intruders. Human contact is minimal; people get their gossip from the newspaper, idle chat from the radio, news from the television.

Before going to bed, the Johnsons check that their home is secure. Over the front door, they have fitted a heavy iron security grille in a steel frame. Iron bars are set across the fire escape. They are safe.

At 3.30 a.m. the couple wake in fright. Smoke is filling the flat. They bang on the walls to raise the alarm but very quickly the fumes overcome them and they are unconscious. Firemen arrive swiftly, in time to save them. But they cannot get through the locked security door. It is metal, and massive, and has been fitted by the Johnsons against council regulations to keep out intruders. It takes five minutes to smash the hinges. By the time the firemen find them, the couple are both dead.

Watching television later, tenants on the estate see the real-life drama and tragedy of the Johnsons' death unfold on the screen. The couple had been murdered. Someone had poured petrol through the letterbox, thrown in a lighted rag and run away.

The tenants hear their homes being described to strangers

throughout the city. It all sounds familiar, a formula backdrop for some TV underworld thriller or an agitprop drama.

The Johnsons lived in a twenty-storey tower block built in the 1960s. It is called Pinter House. There is even a caretaker. He tells journalists hours after the murders that there have been several arson attacks in the area lately.

London, 1989. The seventeenth floor of a high-rise block. Inside their private apartment, a young couple check the smoke alarm before going to bed. There is an intercom link to the communal entrance and a direct line to the porter at reception. The service charges also secure the comforting bark, carried up from private gardens below, of a well-fed Alsatian on the end of a well-fed guard.

The tower block was sold for a song by the local authority a year ago. Soaring maintenance costs and dwindling resources, rate-capping, cash limits and pressure to privatize finally forced the housing authority to sell. Government loan charges (the central Government mortgage) will, however, continue to run to the end of its sixty years. The forced sale price will nowhere near cover the outstanding balance of borrowing, which will continue as a rate debt burden well into the next century. Desperate councils may dispose of unwanted housing estates for as little as £1 in order to secure much-needed development, but the repayments remain.

The private developer has, meanwhile, transformed the tower block. He has installed new services, repaired the fabric of the building, redesigned entrances, landscaped and enclosed the former 'public space', redecorated and carpeted the interior, reclad the exterior to smarten it up and signal investment. If he's clever, he will have appointed an architect as project manager to make it all as cost-effective as possible.

This is the high life. Manageable homes for high earners with time at a premium. Cleaning and maintenance contracts come with the lease. Residents have access to a communal gym and a communal garage; indeed, are part of a new community, the kind dreamed of by the early proselytes of the modern movement. Here, everyone is cared for, lives comfortably, shares common interests (equity appreciation, fitness, the visual arts) and has a tangible stake in their own environment.

This is community architecture – small 'c', small 'a'.

The developers who buy up sad old high-rise blocks, tested to destruction by years of arm's-length management by local councils, know that theirs is the only possible answer for a public sector as marginalized as the concept of mass housing itself. Landlord and tenant both are stigmatized by the lingering death of large council estates where the received municipal wisdom of callous disinterest is amplified in the wanton behaviour of the wilder elements in this synthetic 'community'. Places like Broadwater Farm estate in Tottenham, the scene of such savage conflict during the riots of 1985, were once the battle hymns of architectural modernism. Now they are the battlegrounds of the modern world, where bullies and vandals are beyond the control of the police force.

If architects are held responsible for creating concrete jungles, is it any wonder that the profession is deemed guilty of drafting the law of the jungle which now administers them? Blaming architects for the problems of public-sector housing is like cursing Issigonis when someone writes off your Mini. The designers of public housing when it was fashionable may have been under the lash of unit quotas and cost yardsticks, but they had to design in the belief that what they were doing was architecture for a community. They were men and women with principles, often unswerving in their belief that modern architecture was a revolutionary art, one which would give dignity to its users and bring liberation to the space age.

It is worth reflecting that in 1961, the year Yuri Gagarin became the first man in space, there were 14.1 million households in Great Britain. Of these, more than 3 million (over 21 per cent) had no inside water closet. A further 999,500 households had no exclusive access to a WC. In the early days, heritage had nothing to do with preserving slums. The articulation of modern ideals lay in decent, definable housing standards and an end to the iniquity of New Elizabethans living like incidental characters from a Victorian novel.

Once councils had built the estates, a statutory duty to house had been discharged. By the end of the 1960s, the party was over for mass public housing. The binge had been organized by the government of the time; all the local authorities had been invited and, with sizeable subsidies available to those who built high and fast, the first round, as it were, had been on the house. But nobody knew when to stop, and it was the councils themselves who had to cope with the lingering hangover. Crippling interest rates stretched years ahead, shoddy workmanship matured into cancerous defects. The word 'cutback' entered the municipal vocabulary and stayed there. Estate management was virtually nonexistent. The aspirations of social development evaporated under the heat of a new realism and were replaced by value for money.

We live in an age more pragmatic than that which launched the post-war building boom. Architects and planners have come close enough to universal ideals to know that they are almost certainly unattainable. Now, specific schemes which seek to restore human pride in the environment are offered as exemplars, isolated little beacons of hope in a gloomy urban wasteland. A row of terraced houses in Macclesfield, or even a new village for the Duchy of Cornwall – each brings its own environmental solution and its own perimeter fence. Neighbourhood schemes have triumphed through enterprise and entrepreneurialism, not through social policy; the DoE helps those that help themselves.

Demographic trends during the last century have utterly changed the nature of housing needs. In 1891, the average number of persons per household was 5.32. Today, it is just over 2.5 persons. Then, there were bigger families, but a much smaller population. By 1901 the total population of the United Kingdom had reached 38,200,000. The Central Statistical Office calculates that a century later, in 2001, the UK population will have crept to 57,700,000.

The number of people aged sixty-five or over is nearly five times greater now than in 1901. The percentage figure is set to grow as we move into the twenty-first century, though more slowly because of low birth rates in the 1920s and 1930s. There will be a dramatic increase in those aged eighty-five and over, who are projected to make up 11 per cent of the elderly in 2001 compared with just over 8 per cent now.

More than one-third of our old people live alone, another third with an 'elderly spouse' only. The proportion living alone increases with age, to more than a half among the over-eighty-fives. Those lucky enough (or with no other choice but) to live in sheltered accommodation are becoming more numerous. The nuclear age brought with it the nuclear family: as the numbers of old people increased, sheltered housing schemes proliferated. The concept of elderly relatives encamped in a secure environment, with centralized services, alarm systems and integrated community spaces, gained momentum. Instead of being made to feel a burden on their families, old people were encouraged to feel part of a new 'community' of pensioners who naturally graduated from an independent life to one lived in a cared-for commonality. The safe ghettos of residential homes for the elderly established some basic principles for trouble-free living: group people according to age and status, provide a definable and enclosed environment, design in defensible space around individual units and install permanent staff and security systems. This template has now been appropriated to define living standards in the most sought-after apartment blocks in London's Docklands, where the young and childless affluent enjoy the same standards of safety and maintenance.

The right to a well-cared-for urban environment in which people can peacefully co-exist without the constant fear of burglary and attack can and should extend beyond these two groups at opposite ends of the demographic spectrum – the feeble old and the young rich – and it is part of the architectural profession's role to convince both the public and private sectors of the massive levels of investment currently needed in our towns and cities. We have never shirked this. Often our advice has been misappropriated by those seeking cheap and easy solutions, or compromised by inadequate funding. But whatever styles architects choose to adopt, a kind of Hippocratic oath binds them to their art; an art defined by people and made nonsense without them.

The technological revolution which delivered modernism to an uncomprehending world should never have obscured the most fundamental link in the architectural process: that between the architect and the building user. When architects and users become separated, intervening forces of expediency scramble the format.

The art of architecture can never be about the fronts of houses; it has to be about what a building does for the people living or working in it. We are not, as some of the Prince of Wales's adherents seem to think, exterior designers. We discover ways to shelter people.

Architects invented sheltered housing, just as they have the vision and skill to design the new homes which are needed to serve the post-industrial family. The profession carries a national responsibility for both the science of housing and the art of home-making. Architects as a group must now *instruct* government on behalf of society on the forms of social housing required to re-establish public concern.

And there must be newer and newer ways of sheltering people, as society finds newer and newer ways of defining itself. When the Prince of Wales talked about, or is said to have talked about, a divided nation, he expressed the fears of many in the uneasy aftermath of inner-city riots and high unemployment; fears that the country is being riven by economics into a rich South and a poor North, into suburban rich and urban poor. This trend has been evident for some time, along with more subtle forces of demographic change. The society which seemed in so much turmoil back in the 1960s now looks, at this distance, considerably more homogeneous. The sexual revolution, the major inroads made by the women's liberation movement on a world shaped and controlled by a group known cryptically to their adversaries as WHAMs (White Heterosexual Able-bodied Males), the advent of mass-produced and widely available oral contraceptives, an explosion in the number of divorces (Great Britain now has the highest divorce rate in Europe) and the de-stigmatization of illegitimacy (far fewer illegitimate children are now put forward for adoption, while the number of registered illegitimate births has increased) have all conspired in the fragmentation of our society. The proportion of people living in one-parent families has more than doubled since 1961.

And we are continually reminded of our duty as able-bodied designers to serve the needs of those who aren't. Increasing awareness of the need to make buildings accessible for the disabled is due in part to the strident campaigning by the RIBA and architects generally. Indeed, the Prince of Wales acknowledged this in 1984:

I know that many architects are now fully aware of the needs of disabled people and of their understandable desire to live as near 'normal' a life as possible. Because of this increasing awareness on the part of architects and planners I am sure that there will be considerable progress in this field. But there is a particular problem to overcome and that is the fire regulations which apply to all public buildings. Selwyn Goldsmith wrote about this in his *Designing for the Disabled*, which the RIBA helped initiate in 1961. Referring to building hazards to disabled people and the demands that exist for strict controls, he says, 'For those who administer fire regulations the easy way out is always to say, "Yes, we must choose more controls because we are bothered about people dying." The more difficult alternative is to say, "No, we shall not, because we are concerned about people living." '

Five years later, in 1989, the Prince seemed less convinced of the probity of the architectural profession and, at an awards ceremony to salute builders who had made their housing schemes accessible to the disabled, suggested that architects and designers lacked understanding. He urged architects to spend a day in a wheelchair to discover for themselves the problems faced daily by the disabled. Defending architects' record of concern and lobbying for the disabled, Peter Carolin, editor of the *Architects' Journal*, suggested the prince spend a year in an architect's office.

If the tenets of community architecture are to mean anything at all, they must apply to everybody and not just to isolated streets and estates where small groups of people are able to improve the status of their neighbourhood by hiring an architect to beat everyone else to the meagre grants available. If we are serious about improving the standards of housing and the quality of environment for our people – whether our people are Peruvian peasants or Liverpudlian unemployed – then we must put up some serious money. Smuggling small groups of people across the economic border to property ownership is all very well, but if architecture is to remain relevant as a social force, it must remain united in its aims. A diversity of styles is the profession exercising individual free choice. But there must be no diversity of purpose. *Sheltered housing for all!*

17
New King for
a New Millennium

The twenty-first century is due to start early, as most centuries do. The *fin de siècle* we are heading to has immeasurably more significance than most because it is at the threshold of a new millennium. And if there is not, by the turn of the century, a new king of England, the celebration of a new age will certainly endure until the next coronation.

Architecture, in common with all art forms, will discover a unity of purpose as we near the year 2000. With our vision currently focused on the middle-distance objective of a unified Europe in 1992, the further horizon seems far off, yet in reality it is almost upon us. The festivals and expos of the past will pale beside the global celebration the new millennium will inevitably occasion.

Just how far the art and artefacts of the tail end of a century subsconsciously reflect a kind of chronological fatigue, a yearning to get on with the new, is a matter of some speculation. Nevertheless, the morphology of our urban landscape cannot fail to be influenced by the need for new forms in a new scientific age. We simply cannot go to the Millennium Ball wearing the threadbare rags of post-modernism and neo-classicism. It will be a glittering event.

The millennial vision will produce commemorative buildings and monuments throughout the world. Every town and village will want to have its own. By the mid-1990s, a fresh architectural debate will be roaring over the kinds of built forms we want, both to take us in to the twenty-first century and to leave behind as worthy symbols marking the last decade of the second millennium AD.

This refocusing will be compelling and welcome, and it will, I suggest, result in a reaffirmation of the principles of an architecture shaped – and created – by technology. The grapeshot of late

Elizabethan pluralism will be replaced by the single cartridge of neo-modernism.

It is almost as difficult to characterize Elizabethan architecture as it is to define Carolean architecture. The period 1953–90 in Britain seems to divide, more or less, into three broad movements.

First came the industrialized phase, framed by the Festival of Britain and Ronan Point: the late and mismanaged application of modernism and expediency. Then, through the 1970s and into the early 1980s, the transitional period of neo-vernacular, which gave us all a salutary indication of what happens when architecture is designed by planners. The last phase, in many ways the richest, is one of stylistic diversity; but the pluralism of the playground cannot go on for ever, and already the bell is ringing.

Reports of the death of British modernism have been greatly exaggerated. Modernism did not die with the collapse of Ronan Point, though architectural innocence may have. Britain had already seen the effervescent, though brief, flowering of the new brutalism, whose constellated stars are like a modern pantheon for architects who have kept the faith. Alison and Peter Smithson, James Stirling and James Gowan, Denys Lasdun; these and other pioneers were responsible for a peculiarly British form of post-war modernism which, like its European counterpart, was possessed by the challenge to construct moving relationships out of brute materials, as the great architectural commentator Reyner Banham put it.

Describing the Smithsons' 'House of the Future' project of 1956, Banham writes in *The New Brutalism*:

The House of the Future was, in a sense, a restatement of Le Corbusier's Citrohan/Citroen pun; a house built like a motor-car. But those aspects of automotive technology which Le Corbusier had rejected as un-architectural (notably technical obsolescence and physical expendability) were accepted by the Smithsons as an inevitable part of the mass-production situation, and were fused by them with one of the most traditional of architectural conceptions, the patio-dwelling. The design had been commissioned for the annual 'Ideal Home' exhibition in London, and what the Smithsons offered to baffled (but often enthusiastic) visitors to the exhibition was a simple box without external windows, and a door on only one side, so that the three other sides could be packed hard up against other similar buildings to give high residential densities even in single-storey developments. All the rooms were lit from continuous glazing looking into a small oval patio in the centre, the height of the roof being varied in a continuous curve to give daylight-factors suited to the use and aspect of the rooms around the patio ...

... The House of the Future was therefore styled as much as it was designed. A complete aesthetic of panels and joints (avowedly modelled on automobile practice) was devised, and the exterior even boasted a certain amount of token brightwork that underlined its affinity to the chromium styling of a car or, indeed, the domestic appliances inside. Even the possibility of an annual model-change was entertained.

The contemporary fashion for disguising the uncompromising forms of the modern movement can only partially succeed: covering the South Bank with retail marzipan and icing cannot hide the original purity of inspiration. Modernist architects in this country over the last two decades have been not dead but simply dumb, circumspect. They went into hiding after popular fundamentalists, brandishing copies of the Essex *Design Guide*, sentenced them to death for having read the Satanic *Vers une architecture*.

There is no doubt that the heroic phase of the modern movement would have worked itself through as a theory had it not been for the Second World War. After the Nazis closed the Bauhaus in the chill wind which followed Hitler's accession to the chancellorship in 1933, the theoretical speculation about new architecture was at its critical point. Very few real buildings had been built to the Corbusian theory: there had been the showcase expos and the set piece one-off houses, but no real attempt at building on any scale at all. If the war had not intervened, the thesis of modernism would have had its *auto-da-fé* earlier. The systems would have been taken up and tried out on an international audience. Some aspects of modernism, like the flat roof, would have failed. We could have seen cheap mass housing constructed quickly for political ends - on the same basis as Ronan Point - but on a scale inconceivable now. The stock would have degraded quickly, modernism would have been found wanting, and the world would have said to the Walter Gropius fan club, 'Thanks for nothing. Back to the drawing board.'

There would have been a large number of modern movement buildings in this country in the late 1930s. Not classical-modern but pure modern. The war suspended testing of the theory and kept it on the pages of polemical texts written by modernists in exile from a world which was concentrating its mind on how to destroy, rather than create, buildings.

But modernism was perpetuated in theory and the faith of its adherents deepened. Young architects were among those who landed on D-Day on the Normandy beaches, with copies of *Vers une architecture* in their knapsacks. They had five years of frustration. No architects were designing to build anything of any real peace-time significance during the war. My father was among those who qualified just before the outbreak of war and was immediately rushed out to the Middle East. He spent five years there, as an architect, his alert intellectual abilities now brought to bear on airstrips and shelters in the desert and gun emplacements. He learned a lot about reinforced concrete and management, though – architectural commissions had been replaced by orders to organize 500 men to build a landing strip for a Lancaster in three days. Bigger and bigger moulds were dug in the sand to cast the concrete.

When the war ended, these young men who had been fired with modernism and hardened by the rigorous training of militarily-controlled and highly functional building, returned flaming with desire to build, literally, a better world. All the architects had been consolidated within the Royal Engineers and their skills had been narrowly directed. Peacetime scattered them far and wide across the British Isles, Europe and America. Travelling round the country today, I am constantly amazed at the number of architects practising in areas where they were born and grew up. The war completely disrupted this geographical stability. In 1945, the old concepts of 'home' and 'community' had been swept away. My father collected his discharge papers, spent a week at the Grosvenor Hotel with my mother and bought a copy of the *Architects' Journal*. The back pages were full of jobs; a depleted profession welcomed them back with open arms.

Those who had stayed during the war had occupied themselves between air raids with planning New Britain. In 1943, two separate masterplans for rebuilding London were exhibited in a 'Britain Can Build It' spirit. The pioneering MARS (Modern Architectural Research Group) had relaid London: a central metropolitan core was flanked by linear industrial zones served by outlying residential districts and public parks. The Abercrombie Plan proposed massive slum replacement and planning zones. The reality was to be more pragmatic. The architects pulled out the worn copies of Le Corbusier from their khaki knapsacks and said, 'Look, we can do it. These ideas aren't new. It's been ten years since the Bauhaus was closed.'

But the scale of the profession's ambition matched that of the Corbusian urbanism itself. It works well on the ribbons of roads leading into Los Angeles, but when you try to put it in Tamworth, the scale looks all wrong. And in America the modernist theory, whipped along by the Bauhaus émigrés themselves, did develop during the war. They had the money to go on experimenting with new techniques not just theoretically but practically; there were seemingly endless supplies of fuel. Buildings could be properly built and properly heated. Modernism was made to work because energy systems and air-conditioning were affordable on the Corbusian scale. Here it was austerity and rationing. British modernism didn't die; it simply fell asleep from waiting too long.

By the 1970s, 'modern' already had an old-fashioned ring to it, a stubbornness which modernists themselves were obliged to emulate. You simply couldn't talk about it because nobody took you seriously. It was like trying to put over your point in a tie-dyed kaftan and 32-inch flares.

Architecture and the public have never been on speaking terms in this country since the Festival of Britain. And even that last conversation had an unbearable poignancy.

'Well, what do you think?'

'Fantastic!'

'You wait, this is just the start.'

'Great. What's next?'

'Well, must dash . . .'

'And will the fairy lights be here for ever?'

'Look, I'll drop you a line . . .'

What was next, of course, was nothing. And after nothing, Next.

From a basic modern world to a co-ordinated one, in twenty years. But post-modernism, as its very name suggests, is an aberration, an absence of being. If rational and universal truths exist in architecture, we need to state them now. For post-modernists, the referential themes are defined by irony: modernism had been born, and post-modern art was a post-natal denial. It is harder for the classical revivalists, for whom modernism is a ghastly vision of the future: they are still sitting at the ante-natal clinic cursing their luck and wishing they'd been more careful. It is hardest of all to believe in the present, like trying to see a painting with your face pressed against it. But I believe we are still in the neo-natal ward and that the infant modernism, born so prematurely and with so deficient an immune system, is thriving in the incubator. Before you know it, she'll be toddling round and talking.

The quixotic campaign for community architecture has divided architects against themselves. The challenge for neo-modernism is rather to create a community of architects once again, one whose individual predilections are sublimated in a common cause. The force for change will come, as expected, from the young. There is something about the architect's 'coming of age' which puts the profession out of step with other vocations but strangely in tune with monarchy. An architect, like a prince, doesn't really grow up until the age of forty. By that time, ideas about style and practice have matured. But they are also out of date. This time-warp does not similarly affect, say, barristers or doctors, who can attain a professional acceptance much earlier in their careers. Architects, having waited so long to be taken seriously, reach the age of forty and wait for life to begin. Many of us, by then, have allowed our ideas to become entrenched and immovable. We should take our cue from our buildings.

If, as seems inevitable, buildings of the early twenty-first century are to be more flexible and adaptable, so then should we. If we are to be a Britain of vision we must agree to disagree about the past. We can love or hate Victorian Gothic or prefabricated 1960s high rise. The argument is historical. But we must achieve a consensus on the New World. By the time we enter a single European Market, it will be exactly 500 years after Columbus's journey of discovery. Do we really want to sail into the third millennium when we can fly?

In the zenith of post-modernism is its nadir. I just knew its days were numbered when I came upon a recent addition to the London office boom. There were these huge Georgian windows, 'mega-windows' probably, halfway up a blank marble façade. It was so lacking in any kind of warmth, or humour, or wit. When references can be used like that, deployed so wilfully, they have become worse than boring: they have become old-fashioned. This office building was a cenotaph on which was written, 'That's all, Folks!'

One of the Prince of Wales's favourite examples of modern architecture – and one of mine – is Michael Hopkins and Associates' Mound Stand at Lord's cricket ground. It is simple, elegant and thrilling. The stretched-roof structure shows great skill and imagination in its design, and is a testament to the freshness that technological ideas have beyond their time – Buckminster Fuller and Frei Otto were pioneering stretched-roof systems thirty years ago. Compulsively simple ideas about the way buildings are put together take an age to become in any way acceptable. I bet the Minoans had terrible trouble trying to sell the lintel at first.

When I was a student at the Architectural Association, with Peter Cook as tutor, there were incredible schemes emerging. Archigram were drawing walk-in cities and plug-in cities, cranes everywhere, buildings with guts on the outside. I didn't think for a moment that I would ever see anything like the Lloyd's building in my life. The whole idea of buildings like that was a complete science-fiction fantasy. Theoretical speculation today gives little clue as to what buildings will be like in the early Carolean period.

I suggest, however, that there will be a conspicuous resurgence of industrialized building and prefabrication as we get nearer to the millennium. The need for a few simple world images for this world event will inspire simultaneous architecture on a massive scale. Another factor is that it is unacceptable to consider for much longer the idea that large quantities of large buildings will be made of bricks laid by men in the same dimensions as those hundreds of years ago, and to a similar time-scale. We can now put up a wall in an afternoon where one made of brick would have taken a week; and technology can make it work. The brick will remain a powerful symbol of cultural continuity and will last for some time as a facing material or as a detail device; but the lavish use of the component in brick cross-walls, which was a feature of the Lillington Street housing scheme, must end. Its role will become more and more that of a referential gesture.

We should curse technology less and human error rather more in our rereading of the last industrialized building period. Go into the architectural schools now and you will see a widespread revival of interest in modern technology. Among young architects just starting in practice there is an unprecedented eagerness for the new. In our practice, all the architects under thirty are perfectly happy not to have a drawing board. I asked one of them how his working conditions could be improved and he said, 'Chain me to a CAD terminal.' CAD – computer-aided design – is no longer a novelty. The notion that the computer is an 'aid' or a tool, like a 3B pencil or a Rotring, is out of date. We are moving into an era of *computer-generated* design.

We have recently completed a scheme for a hotel in Islington that was generated by computer. It involved the most comprehensive use of the technology we had tried so far, and we found ourselves doing things that simply would not have been possible without computer-generated images. The roof we put in was a complicated paraboloid. With the computer, you simply call up a flat grid, tweak it, and glide it into the building on screen. All kinds of geometry are possible. The wide-span roofs of the Festival of Britain and the vast skeletal domes of Buckminster Fuller had to be drawn, incredibly laboriously. The maths was complex – straight lines crossing endlessly at critical points to produce curves. A computer just does it. Like *that*.

A computer is regarded as an aid because the ideas still originate in the mind of the architect. But any architect will tell you that serendipity plays an important part in the creation of any building touched by inspiration. Finding, by accident, just the right combination of process, material and design is not an exact science in any dynamic art. Indeed, the success of any scheme depends in part on its finding its own voice, its own individual response within a genre.

We are approaching the stage at which the computer generates design options through its own ecumenical laboratory of ideas. The parallel is the use of synthesizers in music. Their original function was to fabricate synthetic sounds and then, as the technology became more and more sophisticated, to clone them. The menu of sounds now available to professional keyboard players is so oceanic in its scope that while they must still play the notes, the sound itself may be a completely new combination of constituent sounds. This new sound may be of a kind – may sound like a horn or a full string section – but it is singular, it is unique. The computer offers world-corporate building forms, with every one different. It takes 100 years for a row of identical terraced houses to 'wear in', to become a collection of picturesque and idiosyncratic homes. A once-uniform grey slate roof dips and undulates, grows mottled and stained with age to produce an individual and singular contribution to the townscape. We must now aim to devise single processes which offer a broad palette of shade and colour, an architecture which exploits mass production *and* provides individual voices within the chorus. Let it be a living spectrum of colour, though, and not shades of patina. We should be using the paintbox of youth, not the filters of age.

We must not repeat the mistake of imagining that there can be a revolution overnight in the way that people regard new technology and new materials. There is a natural resistance to change in Britain which must be acknowledged; a genuine preference to have buildings clad in natural materials. The modulation of built forms from the familiar and vernacular – from the second millennium – into the new and contemporary third millennium must be taken at a pace which does not leave people gasping for breath. The neo-modernist revolution must be Fabian in character. And the change must also be part of an international movement which looks up from the national huddles of vernacular styles to a new colloquialism, the world colloquialism of a satellite age.

We clothe our buildings in much the same way as we clothe ourselves. The technology is available to provide us all with those one-piece polyester suits that science fiction writers, back in the 1950s, predicted we would all be wearing by now. Instead of surging here and there in our Mr Spock zip-ups and matching bootees, however, we still want pure new wool and fresh cotton. The architect of the first British building on the Moon will probably attend the opening ceremony in a Harris tweed jacket. We cherish warm and tactile building materials in the same way, constructing innovative built forms and then cladding them in Vernaculite. Indeed, we are still constructing extremely uninnovative built forms to start with. This wall in front of me must be about 1 foot 3 inches thick. From the outside in, there is a layer of sand and cement render, brickwork, a cavity wall that isn't because it's filled with insulation, concrete, blockwork and plaster. The same structural and thermal performances could be achieved by a wall only 2 inches thick.

The intelligent wall is just around the corner. It will be ubiquitous in cities by the early twenty-first century. Buildings can now be clad in super-thin envelopes which are able to change their thermal conductivity, translucency and even their external colour. As the days and seasons modulate, so too will the walls. Buildings will have a different outfit for all occasions. Our cities, considerably more lush with greenery as part of a world-wide planting exercise, will be like kaleidoscopes in slow motion. The architect Robin Spence's design – runner-up in the 1989 competition for a British Pavilion at the 1992 Seville Expo – offered a breathtaking idea. His building used an external skin incorporating movable louvres controlled by sound. The external appearance was generated by the *music* playing inside. As the mood and character of the music altered, so too did the building.

Artificial stone can do things which are unachievable in natural stone: it can turn corners, be fashioned into mouldings in ways unimagined ten years ago. Old materials are much more labour-intensive: the massive output of brick-built vernacular homes as a proportion of new housing in the 1970s was inextricably linked to the availability of a workforce at a time of escalating unemployment. The current construction boom has created a shortage of labour in the building and construction trades, a factor that must bear on the way our buildings are going to look between now and the end of the century.

Old methods and traditional materials are abusive of human time. We can dig the clay to make the bricks in Bedford, quarry the granite in Aberdeenshire; Portland Stone is an indigenous material. We are close to these materials because they are close to us.

There are powerful cultural arguments for retaining old materials in our repertoire, just as there are reasons for keeping old and new forms in any art: after an exhibition of Jackson Pollocks you *need* to see some figurative art; after three hours of Stockhausen you *need* a Bach minuet. There are powerful practical reasons, too, for moving into new bulk-buy materials with caution. New forms of complex external skins for buildings, for instance, rely heavily on petrochemical compounds and are therefore subject to the global tides of a world economy. The ascendancy of the Green movement, championed by architects, will make drastic alternations to the way we specify materials for construction. A mid-term stabilization in supply and cost could radically alter attitudes towards the new methods.

Architects have to face the challenge of a new era in which it is no longer acceptable simply to design as a prophylactic against the ill-defined Sick Building Syndrome. Arguments over what the syndrome is, and what causes it, have been a little feverish of late. Air-conditioning, modern materials, internal layout of offices, inappropriate technology: all are blamed individually and severally for the amorphous collection of symptoms. Dry throat, nausea, lethargy – the syndrome is open-ended.

We must go further than designing buildings which are not 'sick', however, and design buildings which are 'fit', which positively promote the well-being of those who use them. Buildings must be healthy and athletic; they must be designed for longevity. Clients are beginning to realize the long-term advantages of life-cycle costing, which plots the economic cost of the building beyond the construction cost to include maintenance and regular 'check-ups'.

While the more pragmatic forces of destiny will conspire to

shape the forms of twenty-first-century architecture, the stylistic debate will continue to run on parallel lines into the next millennium. Classical architecture is currently popular because it is currently fashionable. It is the power under the throne. However, despite classical architecture's timeless quality, the recent neo-classical revival will appear as the merest blip on the graph by the year 2000.

Classicism in the modern world is nothing more than a temporary self-indulgence. Even Stravinsky wrote his classical symphony, but he was just working something out of his system, as architecture is today with the latest crop of neo-classical mock-ups. I am increasingly aware of how little genuine public support there is for, say, Quinlan Terry's Richmond riverside scheme. We have seen yesterday already. There is something of the stage-set, something sickly about a classical office block, a classical block of flats, even though Terry's classicism is very respectable and is textbook stuff, in marked contrast to the cheaper end of the market, where you can see the most horrendous travesties.

The neophobes who promote the current classical revival have pushed their luck too far. The decline of classicism into a series of planner-friendly scorchmarks is engendering a backlash from the aficionados themselves.

There was a biting appraisal by the *Architects' Journal*'s Astragal column in 1988 of a mixed development designed by architects Moxley Frankl in Greenwich:

The scheme is remarkably pompous. Classical architects in the past tended to use the pediment sparingly. Its origins as a temple entrance meant that it implied grandeur and concentrated attention upon the part of the building on which it was placed or attached. But here we see a humdrum street elevation furnished with no fewer than six pediments.

Unhappy details abound. The ground floor of the end pavilion which, brick-faced, rises straight out of the ground, has no plinth, no set-back, no base of any kind. The ground-floor arched windows are divided by a central mullion – a classical solecism that appears most strange in a classical composition of such pretension; equally peculiar are the front doors set back and off-centre within the arched entrances. Also the rich constructional details that enliven earlier classical brick structures are absent. Here the walls are of monotonous stretcher bond while window arches are either of soldier course bricks or formed with concrete lintels.

I am not suggesting that the architects would have done better to produce a pastiche of the handsome late-Georgian terrace on the other side of the street – clearly they wanted to create something that is classical yet also of the late twentieth century. I merely suggest that the design would have benefited if they had studied closely the area's rich collection of eighteenth-century domestic architecture. To design a building like this in central Greenwich – with Hawksmoor, Wren and some of London's most outstanding classical terraces nearby – is to invite comparison with the past. It is a pity that the efforts of our age come off so badly.

Tarting up new buildings with arches and pilasters is jumping on a bandwagon which is going nowhere. The new Romantics have achieved the fame of Adam and the Ants and will last as long. It would be interesting to know how many classical schemes are actually on the drawing board now. Fewer and fewer, one suspects. Terry, John Adam, John Simpson and the other meticulous revivalists follow in the honourable tradition of modern masters like Raymond Erith and those who defied modernism to build referentially. Their imitators, encouraged by the PR boost of a royal preference, cannot stay the course. If it hadn't been for the Prince, these people would now be regarded as the outermost lunatic fringe, designing gazebos for the *nouveaux riches* in Leicestershire. It is an obsession indulged and encouraged to ludicrous lengths.

I remember seeing the classical masterplan for Spitalfields drawn up by Quinlan Terry. The very corners of the drawings were furnished with *trompe-l'oeil* corners themselves, curled up to look antique. Even the paper on which these plans are drawn must be made to look 200 years old. This cannot be healthy. The classicist camp followers have twigged that it is no longer necessary to articulate a building if you can dress it up. Behind the classicism are Poggenpohl kitchens and suspended ceilings clashing horribly with doorframes.

It is only a matter of time before some architectural necrophile suggests a pre-classical revival to solve the growing problem of Britain's homeless. How natural materials and mass housing could combine in an excitingly reinterpretative way! Whole estates could be self-built by the homeless following the traditional methods established in the second millennium BC – holes in the ground, a shallow drystone wall and a roof of environment-friendly, bio-degradable hazel branches.

Carolean buildings will be larger in every sense. City buildings will be high density. Third-generation tower blocks – this time designed entirely by architects – will resume the trend for conspicuously high landmark buildings. The grain of cities is being changed most quickly by those entrepreneurial developer-patrons in whom King Charles III must place his trust. The lumps of building at London's Broadgate are massive; King's Cross will see huge chunks of development, with buildings high, deep and wide. They will enclose vast spaces served by sophisticated internal-movement systems – wall-climbing lifts, paternosters, escalators and moving floors. To the deep horizontal plans of the City's new wave of 'speculator modern' will be added the deep vertical grids of atrium feeders. Corridors will go up and down, not across.

The synthesis of form and function pioneered by Norman Foster and Richard Rogers, with services and structure almost indivisible, will have to develop at a faster pace as air-conditioning becomes more problematic. In small buildings you can open the window. In large buildings you have to regulate an entire environment. There are endless problems involved in creating a truly modern world. They are all solvable.

Thankfully, there has been no sociological Big Bang for British architects and the people they serve since 1945. The task is not to build on bomb sites and slum-clearance areas in the old sense. But the challenge is more than providing a pitched roof over everyone's head. We must repair or tear down the new slums and rebuild our cities not in deference to history but in anticipation of it.

18

Bimbo Architecture

Despite what some of Prince Charles's supporters may claim, architects are not environmental pastry chefs. Our task is to create the spaces, both internal and external, which define our towns and cities.

The misconception of architecture as appliqué has been reinforced over the last few years by the nature of the debate, which has been all about the 'look' of much of our new development. In attacking the quality of new building, and especially new urban building, the Prince of Wales has attracted a large measure of support. But the criticisms of the anti-modernists are based almost entirely on the appearance of our built environment, not on how it functions; the users of these buildings are simply not part of the equation. The argument, for many of the Prince's supporters, begins and ends with the contribution an individual building – that is, the outside of it – makes to its surroundings.

This is a legitimate area of concern for both architects and the people they serve. For everyone is a consumer of buildings, whether they like it or not. Unlike music or painting, a film or a play, architecture is mandatory, public and unavoidable. For this reason alone, architecture must mind its manners. It must commend itself to the passer-by as well as serve its inhabitants. But appearances can be deceptive. The axonometric view shared by New Royalists is from a helicopter sweeping over the landscape, an overview. A neo-classical façade looks attractive from a distance because we cannot see that its detailing is poor, its materials are inappropriate and its arrangement fashionable rather than traditional. A heritage centre looks like the real thing from a train because all we can see is the shell. A restored Victorian office block has a born-again brightness which proclaims life when it is, in fact, a mummified carcass.

Façadism grew in popularity during the 1980s as a short cut to keeping two separate groups of customers satisfied. If a client needs several thousand square feet of office space designed to exacting modern standards with wide spans, underfloor cabling, integrated technology and sophisticated energy controls, there are now several options. The client might acquire a city-centre site, demolish the existing building or buildings and build a modern office block. But this could be prohibitively expensive, and if the existing building is of any note, the local planning authority might well oppose its demolition. Those who love it will, rightly, fight for its survival. Planning delays are expensive.

Another option would be not to acquire a city centre site at all, accept that planning permission for a new building will be more readily forthcoming in an enterprise zone, and build a tailor-made office block away from the centre of town, perhaps in a planned office zone where nobody goes except the people who work there. A third option gives you the speed of the second by pretending you have done the first.

All over London now, and Manchester, and Liverpool, in all those inner cities hobbling into the twenty-first century on Victorian crutches, you can see façadism rampant. The exterior walls are being preserved but behind the scaffolding and canvas the rest of the building is reduced to rubble and removed through the back door, loaded on to lorries and driven to the nearest enterprise zone, where it becomes environmental compost. Meanwhile, back at the building site, the Victorian façade is jacked up on steel clamps. As the new building rises behind it, hidden from view, the façade is clipped into place, as if nothing had happened. This is not a living architecture; this is a death mask. It is deceitful, unimaginative and cowardly.

The signal being given by reactionary forces in the architectural debate is that if things must change, they must at least not be *seen* to change. But a large Victorian building was not designed to accommodate modern requirements. When a new building is designed, it is created from the inside out: artistry, budget, consultation and function will determine the internal spaces, generate a plan, turn brief into form. A building of integrity expresses its character in its outward appearance. With façadism, you are working in reverse: the datum is a two-dimensional external wall, a piece of architectural jetsam rescued and used quite brazenly to barricade the past against an assault by the present.

There was a fascinating trend in Milan towards the end of the 1980s in sparing public anxiety during major restoration work on historic buildings. A seventeenth-century church would be surrounded by the usual scaffolding and evidence of men at work, but this would quickly disappear behind a 1:1 scale photographic image of the building's façade, enlarged and mounted on canvas to deputize for the real thing. Tourists were greeted by the ghostly sight of a city square framed almost entirely with billowing reproductions of the real thing. It is only a matter of time before someone discovers how to etch permanently the image of a building on to glass-reinforced plastic cladding (GRP) and then simply give it a good hose down every now and then. History in our cities is becoming the reproduction furniture of our urban landscape.

Where no originals exist, it is necessary to create them. In Chester, where strict conservation rules determine the parameters of development, a new office block has gone up on a sensitive site, surrounded by listed buildings. It is mock Tudor, with exposed 'timbers', a projecting first floor and a steeply pitched roof. We may not be able to tell the difference between it and the real thing from a distance, but is this what we really want for our cities at the end of the twentieth century?

Garden centres and DIY stores that look like the Crystal Palace are *de rigueur*. Indeed, at Crystal Palace there is a hotel proposed by Holiday Inn which won planning permission on the strength of its impersonation of Paxton's original structure, despite the fact that it uses curtain walling and a mirror-glass skin. When we are not replicating the originals, we are dressing up modern buildings with anachronistic bits and pieces from another century: a twentieth-century arch is built into the wall of a reception area in the City of London; a Georgian crypt discovered during excavations is rescued and rebuilt, stone by stone, as a carpet-tiled marketing suite. We pin remnants of the past on to our urban fabric like antique brooches. 'Oh, we don't usually dress up like this', we say to each other. 'It's just that we're expecting company.'

The phenomenal growth in the last decade of tourism and leisure has intensified the retarded view of our country as a heritage museum, a back-lot Britain where the wishing wells are full of foreign currency. History is big business. From the privately owned tip of Land's End to the restored philanthropic housing in New Lanark, the message is, 'If you've got it, flaunt it.' And if you haven't got it, fake it. The important thing is to create a good impression and keep to the brief which has been given us by the new user groups who pump in yen, Deutschmarks and dollars. The way they see us is the way we are; and the way we are is the way we were.

Leisure time is no picnic these days – the assumptions are that people want their heritage animated. Now the clever money is going into a new generation of heritage 'experiences', where the emphasis is on merchandising. The logic is that punters who pay £3 a head to 'experience' exact replicas of the slums t heir parents said good riddance to after the war will also buy a T-shirt for £3 to proclaim the encounter.

It is true that our heritage seemed in mortal danger in the 1960s, when town planning and highway planning charged through cities with an irresistible force. Nowadays, heritage is feeling much better. It is sitting up and is able to talk. The audio-visual systems, the videowalls, the stage lighting and quad sound, the *tableaux vivants* of Manpower Services Commission – drafted youngsters done up like Vikings or Edwardians: this is all designed to sell history as a package. You will soon be able to step into a living heritage museum at Dover and 'experience' a war-time air raid (perhaps the children could compare notes with Granny later on). You can be part of a Norman invasion force as it splashes ashore in 1066. The Bayeux *what*? Tapestry shmapestry.

The English Tourist Board has gone visionary, too. A new initiative called 'A Vision for the Cities' was launched in 1989 by the Government, which these days has a Minister for Tourism. The ETB is plugged in both to the Government's Action for Cities campaign for inner-city regeneration and to the Carolean vision of

Britain with the clocks permanently stopped at ten to three; for the UK tourism industry, which saw a turnover of £15 billion in 1988, sees a big future in the past. The economic attraction is that it generates jobs and wealth by setting up 'tourism development projects' in run-down urban areas. The deal is that tatty old bits of the city are restored and have their 'character' enhanced by comprehensive schemes which repair the fabric of the buildings; the areas are then marketed in much the same way as 'period features' in an estate agent's description of a house for sale. It makes the city feel good about itself, and attracts visitors, who come and go, spend and leave. A ripple of wealth then spreads outwards, upgrading urban life itself.

The distinction between historic buildings and visitor attractions is becoming a little blurred: the buildings themselves are being marketed as attractions worthy of a visit. A well-aimed marketing campaign by the ETB raised the revenue from historic buildings 13 per cent to £108 million in 1987, and the figure is climbing rapidly. Church-visiting tourists outnumber church-going Christians. The contemporary brand of cook–chill heritage has yet to demonstrate fully how capable it is of acting as 'a catalyst for urban regeneration' in the ETB's vision of tourism; or how far historic attractions will remain a series of isolated refurbishment schemes. This is how the Board's director of development described urban renewal in January 1989:

We're not talking about utopia but we are talking about a new type of city. A 'city within a city' . . . bold and innovative design for mixed uses should form part of the scene. With this approach, new niche businesses will prosper and human qualities can be attracted back into the inner city again . . . the government has not hidden its contempt for indecisive local government and it is up to the local authorities, and particularly the Urban Development Corporations, to take up the initiative . . . It is often thought that the private sector will provide the inspiration, and local business does have a vital role in generating energy, enthusiasm and enterprise. But they cannot do it alone. The public and private sectors must work together . . .

The 'Vision for the Cities' campaign acknowledged that the best form of defence – if you are defending heritage on economic grounds – is attack, and ingenuously abbreviated its programme of 'site specific development initiatives' to SDI.

Liverpool's Albert Dock is often cited as an example of how obsolete lumps of our urban landscape can be revitalized. In 1988, around 3.5 million people visited the waterfront development of shops and galleries that the old, redundant buildings now accommodate. It is imaginative recycling and has preserved some fine architectural exteriors. There is a place for sensible reuse of old buildings in any redevelopment of our urban spaces. But the character of our towns and cities should not be rewound and frozen at a point somewhere in the late nineteenth century, tweaked here and there into bijou little cobbled streets full of Sock Shops and souvenir grottoes. We are in danger of creating a stage set for a restoration comedy, of relegating architecture to a point where its function is merely to announce what it cloaks. Whether it is an old façade retained to clad an office building or a jaunty visitors' centre converted from an old farmhouse to channel admissions through the toll gate, the architecture is skin deep. A derelict series of backstreets and crumbling houses can be saved by the local authority, but first the advantages have to be weighed. The buildings can be restored, but what's the return? Unless some economic generators can be introduced, it will be an expensive business.

A private sector partnership is often the most attractive option for the custodians of our heritage. A familiar pattern of 'restore and recoup' is not enhancing but eroding the character of our towns; we are gift-wrapping heritage. The glazed roof over a Victorian street and 'the pavementization' of market squares, with their new-old repro lamp standards and new-old Victorian bollards, combine to produce an announcement that this is a Victorian street or a market square. A worrying level of visual illiteracy means we need to sell our past with ancient lettering which spells out the opening times. The processed past which pulls in the tourists is the result of an arranged marriage between venture capital and nostalgia, a combination of the picaresque and the picturesque.

The glass in bull's-eye windows is a case in point. It is a relic of the good old days, when the circular swirl at the centre of a blowing operation was given away by glass factories as useless; you can't actually see very well through it. Poor people used them as windows in cottages because they could afford nothing better. Both the cottage and the window have become symbols of a picturesque past to which we cling with stubborn affection. The cottages with bull's-eye windows and quarrelled bays are now transplanted to our towns and cities, where they are filled with baubles, bangles and beads for the palefaces who come from across water with chargecard. Architecture in these olde worlde retail quarters is simply the decorative sealant used to glue the old bits back together again. It has a cheerful smile, like that of the young woman on the tour bus now gliding past. Both fade at the end of the day. The transient world of heritage tourism requires a building to last for only a hundredth of a second at f:8.

Architecture is being used like a bimbo at a trade fair, to attract the customers.

The real growth area for bimbo architecture is in retailing, where the trend in the 1980s was for larger and larger units. As the rapid acceleration of out of town centres slowed down, the focus shifted to large chunks of city centres themselves. Festival shopping, themed shopping, the venture capital is flowing into one-stop shopping centres or, as the Prince of Wales calls them, 'retail environments'. Forget your life, come shopping. The effect is like entering one of those 'cities within cities' the tourist board was telling us about. It is glazed in, a mall of multiples, cul-de-sacs full of speciality shops, the niches filled with niche retailing.

In retailing, however, bimbo architecture is on the inside. The MetroCentre in Gateshead is an architectural nightmare. Nobody doubts that the developer, John Hall, has conjured an economic miracle from the polluted wasteland of the North-East. Even his critics acknowledge the depth of his real-estate vision. He believed when all around him doubted and put his money up. He understood the nature of a future market: indeed, he created a market of the future. With all that money and vision, then, why does is it all have to be a lie?

One and a half million square feet of air-conditioned grazing space, the MetroCentre is maintained to a level set by the stainless fast-food franchises, with a similarly high profile for the sweepersup and the washers-down. It is McDonald's with shops, and it has done for architecture what Esther and Abi Ofarim did for popular music, for the accent in bimbo architecture is heavily on the bim. The massive internal space which admits coachloads of day trippers every hour to browse and gawp and spend their way through 1,600 metres of internal streets has been designed not by architects but by a Canadian firm of interior-design retail-environment specialists, who figured, rightly, that what went down well back home – Christmas all year – would go down well here. In the colonies, as it were.

For the Gateshead shoppers the interior designers have created a 'Vision of Britain' that has crossed the Atlantic twice. Here is a giant Alice in Wonderland tea shop with giant Mad Hatter teacups for people to *sit* in, for goodness sake. This isn't Fantasy Island, it's Ecstasy Island. It is an hallucination in wonderland. A glass-reinforced plastic humpback bridge leads over a babbling brook to the village square, an artificially lit antiques market disguised as the retail sector's version of the Ideal Home Exhibition's tacky end. Fake brick, fake half-timbering: it is a set, a stage set. Unreal and unconvincing, the retailers apparently accept that we can't believe in them. None of us is that stupid. What the shoppers know is that once inside a retail environment, anything can happen but it won't hurt them. Cigarette ends and loiterers are cleared away by the men and women in uniforms. This is a fun, leisure, retail, lifestyle experience and it is served by spaces which imitate a rich kid's birthday party in an episode of *Dallas*. It is a machine for shopping in. The MetroCentre sent Patrick Hannay, writing about it in the *Architects' Journal* in January 1988, racing for the exit: 'There is no room here for a child to convert a leftover cardboard box into a Maserati. There is nothing left to chance.'

The atmosphere invites us to pretend, but let us not pretend, for one moment, that this is real architecture. It is ephemeral and disposable. But it is an environment, and being there is a culturally impressive experience in the same way as visiting St Paul's Cathedral is. But whereas one raises our spirit, the other diminishes it, demeans us with its self-conscious frivolity. Going shopping is an elemental activity and the environment in which it is done should be entertaining, challenging, efficient. It should look to the future, as the product manufacturers and merchandisers who fill our shopping centres look to the future.

Style and choice drive the shopping boom. The ones with the spending power have discovered that it is not just the goods on display which are weighed and graded. The new science of retail anthropology experiments on the people themselves in its standing conferences on 'unit throughput' and 'lifestyle dissonance'. The challenge is to get the right people to the right products: we are the white mice in the laboratory maze. What we feel is of less consequence, ultimately, than how we perform.

Just how much bimbo architecture can we take? So much. It has a big smile and a pretty face, but nothing between the ears. It scoops up just enough dressing-up clothes to create an impression. It is 'hi-tech' architecture without the tech and with an exclamation mark after the 'hi'. It says, 'Welcome! Have a nice day!' And the pearly white smile is frozen.

Façadism, which started as a way of disguising new buildings as old ones, has discovered the opposite route. The bimbo as vamp. Or rather, revamp. While the internal spaces of our buildings might not have changed since the 1960s, entrance halls and elevations can be applied like Letraset and changed every three or four years to follow current trends. Modern façadism is now almost a seasonal thing; the outsides of buildings generated not by internal function but by external whim. A non-generative façade is currently regarded not only as acceptable but as desirable; the bimbo wears *haute couture* or a wet T-shirt, depending on what is being sold.

Bimbo architecture is sexless, neuter. Architectural titillation aims to snare all of us in a fleeting affair with an unreal world. Even some of our most imaginative architects eventually sink into façadism under the pressure of inspirational supply and demand. Clip-on contemporary styling is not giving people what they want, it is giving them what other people want them to want. In late-twentieth-century Britain, nobody wants ordinary anything. Architects must be among the first to change all this.

Taking its cue from the expanding cultural empire of America, Britain is in the grip of specialness syndrome. The plain and honest is simply not good enough; it must be beautiful to count. Nobody in *Dallas* is ordinary, therefore nobody in Dorking must be either. Architects find themselves being asked to perform cosmetic surgery instead of design. We are not skin specialists; we are general practitioners.

I have seen the future and the Philistine is in retreat. And by Philistine I do not mean the kind of person who doesn't understand art, but the kind of person who only understands more. Matthew Arnold, in *Culture and Anarchy*, wrote: 'The people who believe most that our greatness and welfare are proved by our being very rich, and who most give their lives and thoughts to becoming rich, are just the very people whom we call Philistines.'

When the piecemeal regenerators of tourism, heritage and retailing yield, as I believe they must, in the 1990s to a more comprehensive urbanistic approach, one which treats the city as a whole and not as the sum of unrelated parts, it will be the quality of our architecture which is paramount, not its sex appeal. Then perhaps the pop historians will be organizing their own coach tours for a last look at the tatty remains of a misguided cultural introspection: bimbo architecture.

19

The Suzuki Approach

There are thirty-six schools of architecture in the UK. Every year, hundreds of young people emerge from the system to become qualified architects.

These are the people who may be shaping the Britain of 2020, under the stern gaze of a seventy-year-old King Charles III. They may, however, just be the people working for the people who shape twenty-first-century Britain. It will depend on the skills they are taught, and how.

Japanese and American companies have seen the writing on the wall. It says, 'Welcome to Britain.' While the British architectural profession has argued with itself throughout the 1980s over how far to limit the numbers of British architects, multi-national interests have been advancing by stealth into the very heart of our construction industry. Canary Wharf, the hottest piece of real estate in Europe, is busy turning upwards of £3 billion worth of capital into a massive business centre. The developers are Canadian, the architect masterplanners are American, the designer of the centre-piece 800-foot tower is American–Italian.

Kumagai Gumi, the giant Japanese contractor and developer, led the first wave of Japanese investment in British property development. Inspired and encouraged by the success of the Japanese motor industry in turning dole queues into assembly lines, the company entered the British market in 1985 and has since developed more than a million square feet of office and retail space here. British architects like the large practice of YRM, who have worked with Kumagai, were impressed by the team spirit central to all Japanese industrial methodology. Yosuke Masuda, chief executive of Kumagai Gumi UK Ltd, observed: 'The basic difference between Western and Japanese companies is that Japanese culture is based on co-operation while Western culture is based on competition.' That may be so, but it hasn't stopped Japanese developers beating the pants off us in the City. While a domestic battle of wills continues over the style of our new buildings, a more pragmatic view is taken by the newcomers.

These are the people who understand what we do not, which is how we are. They see with a dispassionate eye the way the planning system works and the way finance works: the first slowly, the second quickly. Careers turn not on polemic but on planning permissions. Getting high-quality design through the planning system, that's the secret. Getting poor stuff through is easier. The successful American and Japanese architects and developers who work here – the people who taught us words like 'overview' – may see the arcane Dungeons and Dragons world of public inquiry planning with a dispassionate eye, but that eye is always on the ball. This or that local authority will kill six months arguing over planning gain just to have time to think: this or that area can be disturbed only by façadism; this scheme will market only if we can find the Skylon and re-erect it in front of the office block; so-and-so is very *pro-Charles*.

1992 is bearing down on us with speed. It will bring new opportunities for architects throughout Europe to practise their art. On one level a united Europe presents a vision of an invigorating exchange of ideas, a richer, multi-lingual vocabulary of architecture. At another level, it threatens a free-for-all in which the lowest common denominators are widened and lowered even further. Which direction we take depends on the way we learn and the way we teach.

The Prince of Wales is right to complain that, compared to other European nations, we are 'visually illiterate'. He is wrong, however, to suggest that this can be corrected by a return to a more formal teaching system that compels people to draw. His Royal Highness has visited Glasgow School of Art, where, he is pleased to record, they continue to teach measured drawing. Now, measured drawing is the cornerstone of a classical training in architecture: it enshrines the ancient tradition of tyro at the feet of the master. The victim is required to measure with scientific accuracy an existing building (the older the better) and then reproduce it, acanthus leaf by acanthus leaf, in pencil lead on paper. It is highly disciplined and taxing work. The process itself can be deeply rewarding, particularly in the understanding of architectural theory, of harmony and proportion. It concentrates the mind wonderfully. When I was a student, I did a measured drawing of the Gibbs building at King's College, Cambridge; it was like taking a photograph with the shutter speed set at four weeks.

Measured drawing inculcates an ascetic hierarchy as rigid as that of sorcery and an elitist contempt comparable to that felt by classics masters for those who know no Latin. But architecture is not a black art. If we want to celebrate the future in form as well as style, we must look to the young and not the old. And the young need to learn by doing, not by copying.

Architecture students are under enormous pressure at the moment from their elders. For expanding architectural practices, young graduate architects are at a premium. Students spend a 'year out' at the end of their first degree and after their second, working in an architect's practice. They may work part-time anyway during their academic studies to supplement their grant. They may return to that practice full-time when they qualify. Schools are constantly being told that they are the nurseries of the profession, that students must emerge from the educational process with as keen an understanding of business as art. The 'architecture as learned society' lobby complains that education is becoming too biased towards hustling for work and that we should re-establish an academic weight to our courses.

They both miss the point. What we need more than anything – more than business sense and more than erudition – is creative energy. We must teach people not just how to appreciate architecture but also how to make it. At the Bauhaus, learning how it was done meant sawing wood and laying bricks. The principle remains sound, though we should teach construction early – if a class of twenty-eight twelve-year-olds is capable of producing twenty-eight identical hat-racks in woodwork lessons, it is capable of building a wall. By the time students have reached university age and have decided to study architecture, they would, if our general education system were properly tuned, have a solid understanding of both the natural and built environment. The vocational challenge waiting for them would then be one in which they could discover and amplify their own voice, rather than have to listen endlessly to the petrified music of their predecessors.

We need to consider the means by which we could teach architecture through the Suzuki method.

Shortly after the Second World War, Shinichi Suzuki began teaching the violin to small children. His results were impressive; pupils made excellent progress and were evidently in possession of a musical feel and enthusiasm hitherto unknown. Boys and girls as young as four were able to canter through *Judas Maccabeus* and Bach minuets with confidence and brio.

The Suzuki teaching method is more popular now than it has ever been. Its basic premise is simple: that it is better to teach practice before theory. Sight reading and musical science play minor roles in the induction of young people into the art of making music. The young beginner is encouraged to play by ear, play from memory. Scales and arpeggios are introduced gradually as tuition deepens. The Suzuki method is art for art's sake.

Talent must be fostered. And those who teach understand that the ability they must cultivate is an ability not to duplicate but to generate. Everybody has to *jam* now and then. The Prince of Wales may be reassured: architects are starting to return to drawing in a big way, but the drawing is not the kind that requires a classical education. The challenge today is not to replicate a complicated building in minute detail but to tackle a blank sheet of paper with nothing in front of you to copy.

The advent of computer-aided design has led to an inevitable decline in the number of architects who draw in the conventional way, on a drawing board. The electronic revolution has also coincided with fundamental changes in the way an architect works, and in the demands of the client. An architect today is expected not merely to give form to ambition but to stimulate the ambition itself. Drawing should be a creative aid; it's something you do as an act of faith to inspire people, not a secret mystery. You start with a blank sheet of paper and a client who wants to build a hospital: you talk and you draw and you try to establish a critical path from concept to completion. What stops you creating a beautiful hospital with modern and expensive materials and set in a lovely landscape with babbling brooks and an orchard is not lack of imagination but the regional health authority's budget.

Architects are no more immune from their environment than anyone else. The real world dictates that you have a client who pays you to get planning permission. The Americans and the Japanese have done well in this country because they are able to catch the spirit of what is required in a rapidly changing world, and improvise. We need to respond to the challenge with skill and agility, not retreat into a cultural bunker. There is a new eagerness among the young for the unproven. It does them great credit, for the future development of architecture depends on cultivating just this attitude, developing the kind of mind that wants to control, rather than emulate, a computer.

The four essential points in learning to play the violin by the Suzuki method are:
1. Listening to recorded music to develop musical sensitivity.
2. Tonalization: the production of a beautiful tone.
3. Being in good shape: 'Constant attention should be given to accurate intonation, correct posture and the proper bow hold.'
4. Motivation.

There are those who would argue that the first injunction, which requires the pupil to listen to reference recordings, is a learning process parallel to the study of historic buildings. In both cases, the student becomes sensitized by exposure to existing pieces; drawing, as it were, on a common artistic heritage. This is the past in its proper place, showing us how people made buildings and music.

The Suzuki method, however, uses existing music as an inspiration, not as a template. It is of fundamental importance for pupils to feel themselves making progress. To do this they are encouraged to travel light, with the minimum of cultural baggage. It is true that students must copy pieces of music, music which through a communicable medium of dots on lines can be reproduced by anyone who is able to sight-read. But when the Suzuki student plays the reference pieces, by ear, he or she is merely expected to *try hard.* The anonymous violinist on the recordings is Grade 8 or beyond; the beginner cannot hope to equal the standard of playing. What the teacher is looking for is application and the willingness to practise. The student is not expected to use vibrato or achieve the accuracy and clarity of a professional, but is expected and encouraged to aspire to these qualities. And it must be remembered that the Suzuki recordings, initially, are not masterpieces but practice pieces.

A system of education – whether in architecture or music – which puts theory above practice can be guilty of encouraging a short-circuit of the imagination, for a measured drawing of a building reproduces not just a set of basic architectural principles but the subjective twists and turns of the author's mind. Slavishly following and reproducing the individual nuances of an historic building – measured drawing – makes as much sense in terms of developing one's art as a musician attempting to re-create on tape not just a Shostakovitch piano concerto, but Shostakovitch's own performance of it.

The Suzuki architecture student would spend time more profitably *building* something under the watchful eye of a teacher, rebuilding and rebuilding it until it has achieved its own integrity. It is practice, not theory, which makes perfect.

If tyro architects are serious about their chosen career, theory will be absorbed as a matter of course. Art, philosophy, design methodology, technology: the perfect educational recipe has been a contentious issue since I was a student. The debate will go on, but unless we encourage our young architects to leap before they look, there will exist an energy vacuum into which will pour the glutinous certainties of the past.

However hard the Prince of Wales and I try to kid ourselves, life does not begin at forty. It begins at twenty. And those twenty-year-old budding architects will form a vital generation when the Prince assumes the Crown. What they learn between now and then should be a lesson to us all.

20

Neo-Modernism

Amongst the Philistines there was a general nostalgia and yearning for sham pediments, phoney porticos, outworn arches and attempts to camouflage the squalor with pilasters and a parody of colonnades. Against this background, we shocked the strait-laced by launching a crisp, geometric formation that reflected the interests of our time. The new buildings exuded confidence and élan. They presented a disciplined, unaffected simplicity, lightness of touch and elegance; trim, slim, with poise and grace. Such was our gesture of confidence in rationality, evoking a clear systematic order. We had to fight the nostalgia of the mandarins all the way, and we won. We will win again when the country regains the dynamic impulse; since in the long run, truth always wins.

Berthold Lubetkin, at the reopening of his Penguin
Pool at London Zoo, 1988

There are many intermediate shades of opinion about current architecture and its future. They are framed by two diametrically opposed views.

One school of thought is characterized by a kind of collective dread. Its manifesto says that the modern world is on a collision course, that the only principles worth aspiring to are those of the past, that the key to social stability is the reassurance of familiar forms and styles. It is essentially backward-looking.

The other school of thought is characterized by hope. It says the modern world is what we make it, that the principles of the modern movement – which sought to harness the power of techno-logical impetus and innovation – have been obscured by paranoid introspection and the aesthetic pragmatism of the New Caroleans. The positive school of thought says that we must create a new age of discovery in which aspiration, instead of dragging us back, pulls us forward.

We were all born in the twentieth century, a century which gave us, in its infancy, the theory of relativity, twelve-tone music, cubism, *Ulysses*, Marxism and the Bauhaus. We are now at the turn of the century and most people are still baffled by all of them.

The velocity of time itself has meant that we are constantly struggling to keep up with changes, struggling to understand a world evolving under our feet. The influence of Albert Einstein, Arnold Schoenberg, Picasso, James Joyce, Karl Marx and Walter Gropius is felt everywhere, yet the work of the men themselves remains an enigma to most people. Like all those videotape recordings that bank up in the living room waiting to be watched, iconoclastic ideas have piled up in the twentieth century, waiting to be understood. We accept the principle of a live satellite transmission from the Soviet Union without comprehending it.

The triumphs and disasters of the modern world can now be viewed in longshot. It is time to reassess some fundamental arguments in the light of all that has gone before, as progressive societies have always done. Just as it would be utopian and misguided to imagine that an architectural, a construction, revolution is waiting to hurl us into the twenty-first century, so it would be wilfully short-sighted not to recognize that architecture, like the society it serves, must evolve or stagnate. It is easy now, with media hindsight, to see where we went wrong in the misapplication of modernism. It was an episode in history which bequeathed much more, however, than icons and listed buildings. Modernism showed how designers with an international, even a global, view of the way ahead could rally the leading lights of planning, architecture, engineering and social policy to plot a course to a better world. Not a nicer view from the train or the helicopter, not a better street in Macclesfield or a better council estate in Hackney, but a better world. We have lost this world vision, cowed by the marshalled derision both of a nostalgic bourgeoisie and the anti-élitist tribunes.

The styles and techniques of modernism may have been shunted off to some cultural siding, but the universal faith in the future they engendered within the professions is there still, dormant, latent, waiting for a new impetus. The worst crime of modernism was that of naivety; modern architects were struggling to realize building forms beyond their time.

The world has moved on to a period quite alien to that which witnessed the Weissenhof exhibition of 1927. It seems like ancient history now. While the public flocked in disbelief to hear Al Jolson sing to them from a cinema screen in *The Jazz Singer*. Ludwig Mies van der Rohe and the Deutscher Werkbund constructed a showcase suburb of revolutionary buildings outside Stuttgart and said to the world, 'You ain't seen nothing yet.'

But the shock of the new – the rigorous use of repetition, rectangular boxes defying the traditions of built form – has faded. The revolution in the way architects considered internal spaces was interrupted by a war and its aftermath, which created new limits of imagination and new technological channels, from interior spaces to outer space itself via the atomic age, the race for military technology, geopolitical shifts of glacial magnitude, computers, information technology, the mass-communications industry and an orchestral accompaniment in the Western world of boom, slump, recession, boom.

Modernists queered their own pitch to a certain extent, being at once both childish and patronizing. They were childish in their youthful exuberance and unwillingness to pause for thought, let alone doubt. The doctrinaire application of their theories by a succession of ephemeral power brokers in Westminster and the town halls looks utterly brittle now in retrospect. Modernists are also recalled as being patronizing in their arrogant self-belief. Their pronouncements, delivered always in the imperative, seem pompous and irritating and their buildings seem dark and cheerless to a Docklands generation with its pastel colours and light railway.

The intervention of the Prince of Wales has made honourable what would have been considered cowardly half a century ago: the renunciation of the new in favour of the old. It underpins an image of the past with which the British are constantly caricaturing themselves. For now, as we enter the last decade of the twentieth century, nostalgia *is* what it used to be. The New Georgians of Chelsea and Spitalfields live as far as possible like the Old Georgians.

It is no longer enough that new urban developments respect the vestiges of eighteenth-century Britain; they must mimic them. It is no longer enough for social housing to be built in a form expressive of the materials used; it must be made to look like *private* housing, complete with clipped-on, jokey, quirky symbols of a post-modernism which has become both humourless and irrelevant and flaunts an imagination as desolate in execution as in purpose.

While the modern world surges ahead, apparently moving ever further beyond our grasp, architecture has sailed into the doldrums, say our critics. They talk of architecture at the crossroads, but we are idling only because the lights are stuck on red. Articulated by an heir apparent with the common touch and administered by a planning system which prefers formulae to ideas, popular taste demands reassurance, not challenge.

There are signs, however, that the lights are about to flick to amber. The sheer weight of investment in areas like London Docklands has created a pluralist approach to the built environment which is increasingly unimpeded by the need for deference to the past. Many of the new-generation enterprise zones and urban development areas are still dead wastelands. They await the injection of new ideas.

The arguments for aesthetic control look pretty thin in areas of high unemployment. Risk capital has been encouraged to put down new roots in fallow land. These eager new economic nurseries offer rates holidays, tax concessions, enterprise allowances, Treasury underwriting and simplified planning (that is, 'Here's planning permission. Build whatever you like.') They are all offered in a determined attempt to regenerate. Nobody was seriously going to tell a multi-national investor it couldn't mix a broken pediment with mirror glazing. If we are to put down new roots, said the companies, we shall blossom as we wish. Now business is blooming in Docklands. The first wave of development, which showed the energy and speed with which an eclectic fashion for 'fun' architecture could grip not just the area itself but the stuffy old City downriver and countless areas of urban renaissance throughout the country, is yielding to the second, more visionary wave, which will be unable to resist the skills of our best architects. Richard Rogers has a major commission there, for instance. It is a joyous prospect.

Rogers is, for the Royalists, perhaps the most dangerous living architect. He is openly critical of the Prince's intervention. He is a brilliant architect. He is an outspoken champion of modernism. And, most dangerous of all, he is popular. Ordinary people, to the great discomfort of some, like his work. Despite the campaign of vilification which has dogged Rogers throughout his career, whipped up by fogeyish architectural critics who pray for the first signs of rust on the silver, his architecture rallies popular support. His Lloyd's building is not only the most exciting new structure in London's urban landscape since the war; it also attracts up to 2,000 visitors a day. In five years it has become a national institution. Rogers and those who believe, with him, that architecture has a future as well as a past, predict a more dynamic and responsive environment for the reign of King Charles III.

In a speech to the Royal Society of Arts in April 1988, Rogers said:

The failure of modernity is not that of architecture but that of ethics. The crisis we now face is that our scientific and financial potential has outstripped our ethical and social resources. To live in harmony our tremendous advances in science must be matched by an ethically and culturally equivalent development. The scramble for profit and power must not be allowed to erode our civilization and destroy our beautiful planet. Man has created art, philosophy and science. They are the most beautiful, most enlightened and most enduring achievements.

With the advent of modern science we have the option of having all humanity living at a higher standard than anyone has ever known. To achieve this, we must question traditional beliefs, we must stop being defensive of our property, our market, our nations and our point of view. Civility implies living in harmony with the past, the present and the future.

Rogers talks of new scientific and artistic influences made possible by dynamically adaptable polyvalent walls, solar-cell energy systems, photochromism, low-emissivity coated glass, electro-reflective surfaces and the advent of intelligent buildings.

Michael Davies, one of architecture's greatest technological innovators, describes a building of the twenty-first century:

Look up at a spectrum-washed envelope whose surface is a map of its instantaneous performance, stealing energy from the air with an iridescent shrug, rippling its photogrids as a cloud runs across the sun; a wall which, as the night chill falls, fluffs up its feathers and – turning white on its north face and blue on the south – closes its eyes, but not without remembering to pump a little glow down to the night porter, clear a viewpatch for the lovers on the south side of level 22 and to turn 12 per cent silver just before dawn.

There is a growing feeling among the young architects now emerging into the profession that our ideas have become static and outdated. They have no interest in the inherited guilt of the late modernists. They want to build, and they want to find forms that reflect a new reconciliation between art and science. A new interpretation of modernist principles is needed, one which performs the role architecture has always performed in bringing the benefits of a industrial revolution to the ordinary home. If everyone can have a Sony Walkman, everyone can have an energy-efficient house.

Forget post-modernism. It was a welcome attempt to brighten up a Britain on the dole, a Britain which was taking less and less interest in its appearance and needed to get smart. It was architecture for consumers. Now we need a new architecture, a neo-modernism, for the new producers. As patterns of work undreamed of at the height of the manufacturing boom evolve to shape the reign of King Charles, so technology will need to be briefed to cope with new patterns of living.

There's nothing new under the sun; it has to be neo. But if the choice is to be between bowing and scraping our way backwards into the Carolean age with a neo-classicism which ignores new technology or rediscovering economies of scale with new materials and new techniques aimed at sheltering *everybody*, I say let the cause be neo-modernism.

Appendix

COMMUNITY DEVELOPMENT
Enable the user client to develop and organize as a group.
- attend group meetings.
- advise and assist with constitutional and management matters.
- execute social surveys and/or social appraisals.
- set up and maintain project office accessible to the user client.

Project education
Acquaint the user client with the design and building processes.
- develop design and planning aids for user client participation.
- assist the user client in choosing an appropriate building and/or site.
- establish contact with relevant people, projects and information sources to assist the user client.

Feasibility studies
Provide additional resources and skills.
- assist the user clients to argue their case for capital and/or revenue funding.
- prepare business feasibility plans.

Lay communication
Produce information specifically for communication with the user client.
- prepare and distribute drawings, models, programmes, newsletters and questionnaires.

User client meetings
Enable the user client to participate in the design and building processes.
- organize and attend meetings between user client and funding bodies, and other special meetings.
- organize and attend regular strategy and/or steering group meetings.

Special negotiations
Assist the user client in obtaining project sponsorship.
- prepare project sponsorship packs and/or displays.
- make presentations to funding bodies and other sponsors.

– complete grant and sponsorship applications.

Customization
Provide for individual customization within larger projects in collaboration with individual user clients or groups.

Alternative contractual methods
Provide additional services and/or prepare additional information as a result of alternative procurement and contractual methods, such as self-build projects and projects involving semi-skilled labour or self-help.

Operations on site
Acquaint user client with works on site.
– organize individual and group site visits/meetings.
– involve the user client in site and progress meetings.
– set up and operate user client site offices.

Special reports
Prepare information on where funding bodies and sponsors have criteria requiring special compliance procedures.
– prepare special reports and/or carry out additional works due to specific requirements of funding authorities or sponsors.
– prepare reports as a result of events and circumstances that could not be foreseen.

Management and maintenance information
Prepare information for the user client on management and maintenance.
– advise the user client on alternative structures for management of building and assist with implementation.
– provide manuals and maintenance information suitable for implementation by the user client.
– provide post-completion advice on monitoring, updating and revising management and maintenance procedures.

Further Reading

Amery, Colin and Dan Cruickshank, *The Rape of Britain*, Elek Books Ltd, 1975

Architects' Journal

Architectural Review

Ball, Michael, *Economic Change and the British Construction Industry*, Routledge, 1988

Banham, Mary and Bevis Hillier, *A Tonic to the Nation: The Festival of Britain 1951*, Thames and Hudson, 1976

Banham, Reyner, *Theory and Design in the First Machine Age*, Architectural Press, 1960 (reprinted 1980 with new edition)

– *The New Brutalism*, Architectural Press, 1966

– *The Architecture of the Well-tempered Environment*, 2nd ed., Architectural Press, 1984

Berry, Fred, *Housing: the Great British Failure*, Charles Knight, 1974

Blaser, Werner, *Mies van der Rohe: The Art of Structure*, Thames and Hudson, 1965

Building Design

Consolidation of the Housing Acts 1957–1985, HMSO, 1985

Crossman, Richard, *The Diaries of a Cabinet Minister*, Hamish Hamilton, 1975–77

Curtis, William J. R., *Modern Architecture since 1900*, 2nd ed., Phaidon, 1987

Davies, Colin, *High Tech Architecture*, New York: Rizzoli, 1988

Davis, Terence, *John Nash: the Prince Regent's Architect*, Country Life Ltd, 1966

Drew, Philip, *Frei Otto: Form and Structure*, Crosby Lockwood Staples, 1976

Duffy, Francis and Alex Henney, *The Changing City*, Bulstrode Press, 1989

Esher, Lionel, *A Broken Wave: the Rebuilding of England 1940–1980*, Allen Lane, 1981

Essex County Council, *A Design Guide For Residential Areas*, 1973

Fordham, Richard, *Planning Ready Reckoner*, Planning Gain Consultants, 1987

Holden, Anthony, *Charles, a Biography*, Weidenfeld and Nicolson, 1988

Jackson, Antony, *The Politics of Architecture*, Architectural Press, 1970

Jencks, Charles, *Modern Movements in Architecture*, 2nd ed., Penguin, 1985

– *What is Post-Modernism?* Academy Editions, 1986

– *Post-Modernism: the New Classicism in Art and Architecture*, Academy Editions, 1987

– *The Language of Post-Modern Architecture*, 5th rev. enl. ed., Academy Editions, 1987

– *Le Corbusier and the Tragic View of Architecture*, rev. ed., Penguin, 1987

– *Architecture Today*, Academy Editions, 1988

– *The Prince, the Architects and New Wave Monarchy*, Academy Editions, 1988

Joedicke, Jürgen, *A History of Modern Architecture*, Architectural Press, 1970

Knevitt, Charles, *Space on Earth: Architecture, People and Buildings*, Thames and Hudson, 1985

Lasdun, Denys (ed), *Architecture in an Age of Scepticism*, Heinemann, 1984

Le Corbusier, *Towards a New Architecture*, Architectural Press, 1927, translation of *Vers une architecture*, originally published 1923

Lyall, Sutherland, *The State of British Architecture*, Architectural Press, 1980

Morris, William, *News From Nowhere*, 1890

Nuttgens, Patrick, *Understanding Modern Architecture*, Unwin Hyman, 1988

Pawley, Martin, *Home Ownership*, Architectural Press, 1978

Ramprakash, Deo (ed), *Social Trends No. 16*, Central Statistical Office, HMSO, 1986

RIBA Journal, Royal Institute of British Architects

Rogers, Richard, 'Belief in the Future is Rooted in the Memory of the Past', RSA Journal, no. 5388, November 1988, pp. 873–884

Scoffham, Ernest R., *The Shape of British Housing*, Godwin, 1984

Sudjic, Deyan, *Norman Foster, Richard Rogers, James Stirling: New Directions in British Architecture*, Thames and Hudson, 1986

Venturi, Robert, *Complexity and Contradiction in Architecture*, Museum of Modern Art, New York, 1966, Architectural Press, 1977

Wates, Nick and Charles Knevitt, *Community Architecture: How People Are Creating Their Own Environment*, Penguin, 1987

Williams, Neville, *Royal Homes*, Lutterworth Press, 1971
Wright, Frank Lloyd, *The Future of Architecture*, Horizon Press, New
    York, 1953

Index